Hegel's Dialectic

Hans-Georg Gadamer

Hegel's Dialectic
Five Hermeneutical Studies

Translated and with an Introduction
by P. Christopher Smith

New Haven and London   Yale University Press

Originally published in German under the title
Hegels Dialektik, © 1971 by J. C. B. Mohr
(Paul Siebeck), Tübingen.

Library of Congress catalog card number: 75–18171
International standard book number: 0-300-01909-2

Designed by John O. C. McCrillis
and set in IBM Baskerville type.
Printed in the United States of America by
The Alpine Press, Stoughton, Mass.

11   10   9   8   7   6   5   4   3   2

Contents

Translator's Introduction

Contained in this small book are translations of five of Hans-Georg
Gadamer's essays on Hegel. Four of these, Hegel und die antike Dia-
lektik," "Hegel—Die verkehrte Welt," "Die Idee der Hegelschen
Logik," and "Hegel und Heidegger," appeared in a collection of
Gadamer's writings entitled *Hegels Dialektik: fünf hermeneutische
Studien,* which was published by J. C. B. Mohr, Tübingen, 1971. Of
these four, two had been published previously. "Hegel und die antike
Dialektik" appeared in *Hegel-Studien* 1, Bouvier, Bonn, 1961, and
"Hegel—Die verkehrte Welt," in *Hegel-Studien,* supplement 3, 1964.
The fifth essay, *"Hegels Dialektik des Selbstbewusstseins"* (cf. chap-
ter 3 below), which continues the explication begun in "Hegel—Die
verkehrte Welt," appeared together with a republication of the latter
in *Materialien zu Hegels "Phänomenologie des Geistes,"* ed. Hans
Friedrich Fulda and Dieter Henrich, Suhrkamp, Frankfurt, 1973.

The first of the essays which follow in translation here, "Hegel
and the Dialectic of the Ancient Philosophers," is of particular interest because it shows how Gadamer was able to make use of his
vast knowledge of ancient philosophy in reaching a critical understanding of Hegel. Gadamer is guided by two questions: first, why it
is that Hegel, however productive his analyses might be, consistently
misinterprets Plato and Aristotle, and second, why it is that he nevertheless is able to open dimensions of their philosophy which had
remained inaccessible to previous research. In answer to the first,
Gadamer concludes that it is Hegel's insistence on the modern, Cartesian principle of subjectivity which leads him to read things into
the Platonic and Aristotelian texts. In answer to the second, Gadamer
finds that precisely because Hegel breaks through the petrified and
artificial language of eighteenth-century metaphysics and unfolds the
speculative content of his native German, he draws close to the Greeks,
whose philosophy always remained embedded in their native language.
Here a central theme of Gadamer's own thought comes to the fore,
namely, that natural languages are the foundation of philosophical
thought and spoken words, the origin of concepts. Interpretation of
philosophical texts thus implies grounding what is said in language as
it is spoken. Gadamer maintains that though Hegel was not always
entirely aware of it, it was his sensitivity to the philosophic signifi-

cance of natural language which allowed him to perceive the truly speculative content in the dialectic of the ancient philosophers.

In "Hegel's 'Inverted World'" and "Hegel's Dialectic of Self-consciousness" we find two masterful applications of Gadamer's hermeneutical theory. The methods of descriptive phenomenology which Gadamer learned from Husserl are used with all of the latter's "painstaking craftsmanship" to explicate the subject matter of two consecutive chapters in Hegel's *Phenomenology of Mind.* Through meticulous portrayal from all sides, the "things themselves" (*Sachen selbst*) which are being thought about in these texts are made to appear in almost three-dimensional presence.

"The Idea of Hegel's Logic" displays this same hermeneutical technique, the initial concern here being the general idea of Hegel's logical method as illustrated by the first three concepts of the *Science of Logic*: being, nothing, and becoming. Gadamer's phenomenological exposition demonstrates that there is a logical necessity in the development of these concepts, which Hegel does not force upon them, but which lies in the subject matter itself and which his dialectical method is able to display. In this essay, however, Gadamer is also concerned to further develop his critique of Hegel. Here the influence of Heidegger on Gadamer is most evident, for it is Heidegger who first maintained that a course of reflection such as Hegel undertakes in his logical science cannot be carried out in a linguistic vacuum. On the contrary, it always presupposes its foundation in spoken language. Now that argument, as "Hegel and the Dialectic of the Ancient Philosophers" also shows, is basic to both Gadamer's interpretation and criticism of Hegel. It is only fitting, then, that this collection of essays should conclude with a comparative study entitled "Hegel and Heidegger" in which Gadamer shows that by pointing to the way we actually experience language Heidegger was in fact able to refute Hegel's claim that the logical science which unfolds its content within the sphere of reflection is self-sufficient and all-inclusive.

From what has been said one can easily see what particular problems a translator of Gadamer's work on Hegel faces. On the one hand, in faithfulness to Hegel there is the requirement that one be systematic and consistent in rendering Hegel's concepts. On the other, if his concepts, as Gadamer contends, are in fact not at all contrived designators of a pregiven eidetic structure but derive from the German language as it is ordinarily spoken, the translation of them into English should stay as close to ordinary usage as possible in order to minimize any appearance of artificiality.[1] Therefore, in translating Hegelian language I have tried to find a mean between the extremes. For the most part I have kept the translation of a term the same throughout, the chief exception being *Aufheben,* which appears variously as cancellation, elimination, and sublimation. In translating Gadamer, however, my guiding principle has been almost exclusively that of ordinary language usage: rather than trying for a word for word translation, I have sought wherever possible to say in English what one would commonly say on such occasions where the German word or phrase is used. In this way I hope to have conveyed at least some of the natural eloquence of Gadamer's German. For the sake of clarity it was necessary at some points to change the wording of the original text completely. In each case where I have done this I have consulted with Professor Gadamer and together we have sought a way of expressing the sense of the text in question. I am grateful to Professor Gadamer for the help he gave me during the many hours which we spent discussing these essays.

P. Christopher Smith

1. Gadamer's proximity to Austin and the approach of ordinary language philosophy is perhaps best evidenced in chapter 2, note 13, below, where he differentiates between the ordinary use of *falsch* and *verkehrt* in German making precisely the sort of distinctions Austin does. Cf. J. L. Austin, *How to Do Things with Words,* New York, 1970, and chapter 4, note 7 below.

Abbreviations

G. W. F. Hegel

Ph	*Phänomenologie des Geistes,* Meiner, Hamburg, 1952
L I, II	*Wissenschaft der Logik,* Meiner, Leipzig, 1951
Enz	*Enzyklopädie der Philosophischen Wissenschaften,* Meiner, Hamburg, 1959

Roman numerals refer to volume number of *Werke,* ed. "Freunde des Verewigten," Dunker, Berlin, 1832.

Martin Heidegger

SZ	*Sein und Zeit,* Niemeyer, Tübingen, 1960

Hans-Georg Gadamer

WM	*Wahrheit und Methode,* Mohr, Tübingen, 1965

Hegel's Dialectic

Foreword

Hegel's dialectic is a continual source of irritation. Even one who has succeeded in making his way through the tumultuous logic of Plato's *Parmenides* has mixed feelings about it—his sense of logic is offended, yet he feels speculative exhilaration at the same time. I am such a person, and thus early in my career I found myself setting about the task of relating the dialectic of the ancient philosophers to Hegelian dialectic in order to elucidate both in terms of each other. It was not my intention, though, to reflect about dialectic, this method or non-method of thought, in order to reach a final judgment about it. Rather, it was my concern that the wealth of insight which can be derived from and mediated by this puzzling art might be more fully exhausted. For whatever one might say about the questionable logic of dialectic and however much one might prefer the "logic of investigation" to the "logic of the concept," one cannot take philosophy to be simple investigation or scientific research. Philosophy must incorporate within itself that anticipation of the whole which makes our desire to know go round, that anticipation of the whole which lies embedded in language as the totality of our access to the world. And in its thought philosophy must give an account of that anticipated whole. That remains an inescapable desideratum for human reason, even in an age of science which has seen specialization develop in various fields of evermore particular research. Thus, reason cannot afford to scorn what dialectical thought has to offer.

Having been schooled in the sound and solid handicraft of phenomenology and having been confronted with Hegelian dialectic at an early age by Nicolai Hartmann and thereafter by Martin Heidegger, I found myself vexed by the helplessness one feels when faced with Hegel's claim that in his dialectic the idea of philosophic demonstration has been restored. Thus, throughout the decades of my own efforts to think and write, the task stayed with me of bringing the productive unclarity of dialectical thought to life with all clarity of mind, and of learning to exemplify this productive unclarity using the substance of dialectic, the phenomena which are its content. In spite of years of work my success remains modest. It was difficult to maintain the mean between the Scylla of logical objections in the form, "I know better than you," on the one hand, and the Charybdis of unreserved surrender to the dialectical play on the other. And it was even more difficult to communicate what I had succeeded in verifying for myself by retracing the course of speculative thought without making it puzzling all over again. Without the support which the Greek substrate in Hegel's thought offered me my success would have been even less. As it is, I have produced a few essays which hopefully will be of some help in learning to spell out Hegel's philosophy.

1

Hegel and the Dialectic of the Ancient Philosophers

The ancient philosophers developed a method of bringing out the consequences of opposed hypotheses, though to be sure, as Aristotle puts it, they did this without knowledge of the essence or "what" of the things they were dealing with.[1] It is well known that in the eighteenth century Kant's transcendental dialectic of pure reason demonstrated anew the worth of this dialectical method of the Ancients. Like them, Kant saw that reason necessarily involves itself in contradictions. His followers, Fichte, Schelling, Schleiermacher (and Hegel as well), accepted Kant's demonstration of reason's necessary self-contradictoriness in their own thought but, in contrast to Kant, they evaluated it positively. They recognized in it Reason's special capacity to transcend the limits of a kind of thought which fails to rise above the level of the Understanding. They were all aware of the classical origins of dialectic. Schleiermacher, for instance, might even be said to have made Plato's art of guiding a conversation his starting point. Hegel's version, however, will be seen to have a function all its own if compared to the use his contemporaries make of dialectic.

Hegel felt that the essential methodological rigor was missing in his contemporaries' use of dialectic, and, indeed, his own dialectical procedure is entirely peculiar to him. It is an immanent progression from one logical determination to another which, it is claimed, does not begin with any hypothetical assumption but rather which, in following the self-movement of the concepts, presents the immanent consequences of thought in its progressive unfolding of itself. Here no transitions are determined externally. If we follow Hegel's own enjoinder, we should eliminate all introductions, divisions of chapters, titles, and the like from the actual body of the scientific development, for they serve only an external need. Accordingly, Hegel is critical of his contemporaries—Reinhold and Fichte among others— for making the form of the statement (*Satz*) and the fundamental

1. *Metaphysics* M 4, 1078b 25.

proposition (*Grundsatz*) basic to their mode of philosophical presentation.[2] He sees his own procedure, on the other hand, as the true rediscovery of the philosophical demonstration, whose logical form cannot be the one given in Euclid's systematic presentation of geometry and subsequently analyzed in Aristotle's *Organon*. Quite probably, Hegel is seeking to distinguish between this analytical approach and his dialectical one when he writes in the preface to his *Phenomenology*, "Once dialectic had been divorced from demonstration, the concept of philosophical demonstration was in fact lost" (Ph 53).

In substance, this passage could perhaps also be taken to refer to the destruction of dogmatic, rationalistic metaphysics and its mathematical method of demonstration—a destruction which Hegel credits to Kant and Jacobi (XV 543 ff., cf. 608). If we follow this interpretation, the concept of philosophic demonstration would have been obliterated by Kant's critique of the proofs of God's existence and this loss would have ushered in the romantic "nonmethod of presentiment and enthusiasm." However, the context shows us that according to Hegel the concept of philosophical demonstration is not at all correctly understood when it is made to imitate the mathematical method of demonstration. Thus the statement actually makes no reference to the proofs of God's existence based on the model of geometry. It is a quite secular reference to the downgrading of dialectic to a mere preparatory aid, a downgrading very much like the one Aristotle sought in his logical critique of Plato's dialectic. One should not be misled by the fact that in spite of this downgrading of dialectic Hegel rediscovers in Aristotle the deepest speculative truths. For in fact Hegel expressly emphasizes that the procedure of scientific demonstration which Aristotle works out in his logical analysis, *apodeiksis*, is in no way the same as Aristotle's actual philosophical procedure. But, as the case may be, Hegel did not find the model for his concept of demonstration in Aristotle, but rather in Eleatic and Platonic dialectic. With his own dialectical method Hegel claims to have vindicated Plato's way of justifying belief—dialectical scrutinizing of all assumptions. Hegel does not merely assure us of this. On the contrary, he is the first to actually grasp the depth of Plato's

2. Reinhold and Fichte both sought a starting point in which the sides of human knowing which Kant separates in his *Critique of Pure Reason*—sensibility and understanding—could be unified and grounded. That starting point was to be formulated as a "*Grundsatz*" or basic proposition. Cf., for example, Fichte's *Wissenschaftslehre* (*Doctrine of Science*, 1794), Hamburg, 1956. (TRANS.)

dialectic. He is the discoverer of the truly speculative Platonic dialogues, the *Sophist, Parmenides,* and *Philebus,* which did not even exist for eighteenth-century philosophy and which only because of him were recognized as the real core of Plato's philosophy in the following period, which lasted until the feeble attempts in the middle 1800s to demonstrate that these works were spurious.

To be sure, Plato's dialectic too—even that of the *Parmenides*—is in Hegel's view still not "pure" dialectic since it proceeds from assumed propositions, which as such have not been derived from each other according to an internal necessity. Indeed, for his methodological ideal of philosophical demonstration Hegel must rely more heavily upon the overall style of Socratic dialogue—that immanent formation and self-unfolding of thought which he extols in Socrates' guidance of discussion—and less upon the *Parmenides,* the "greatest masterpiece of Ancient dialectic" (Ph 57), or one of the other late dialogues. Without doubt, he saw correctly that the bland role which the partners play in Socratic dialogue favors the immanent consequentiality of the developing thought. He lauds these partners of Socrates as truly pliable youths who are prepared to leave behind all contumacy and flights of fancy which would disturb the progress of thought.[3] To be sure, the splendid monologue of Hegel's own philosophical dialectic realizes an ideal of self-unfolding thought with a much different methodological conception behind it, one which relies far more upon the principles of the Cartesian method, on the learning of the Catechism, and on the Bible. Thus Hegel's admiration for the Ancients is intertwined in a curious way with his feeling that the modern truth shaped by Christianity and its renewal in the Reformation is superior.

The general theme of the modern era, the *querelle des anciens et des modernes,* is fought out monumentally in Hegel's philosophy. Thus, before we begin our examination of the specific uses Hegel makes of Greek paradigms, Hegel's own understanding of the state of this argument between the old and the new should be discussed. In his preface to the *Phenomenology,* Hegel writes,

3. I still believe today that the propaedeutic function which Socratic-Platonic guided dialogue has in paving the way for the idea of "science," a function which I pointed out in my *Platos Dialektische Ethik* in 1931 (reprinted: Hamburg, 1968), is more significant than those adumbrations of *apodeiksis* which F. Solmsen, in seeking the historical origin of Aristotle's *apodeiksis,* has ferreted out in Plato's works. (Cf. *Die Entwicklung der aristotelischen Logik und Rhetorik,* Berlin, 1929, especially pp. 255 ff.)

The form of study in ancient times differs from that of the modern period in that study then was a thorough process of education appropriate for a natural consciousness. In specific probing of each aspect of its existence and in philosophizing about all that occurs, it generated for iteself a universality actively engaged in the whole of its life. In the modern period, on the other hand, the individual finds that the universal is already prepared for him. It would therefore be better to say that in his effort to grasp it and to make it his own he directly forces the inner essence into the open without the mediatory experience of the natural consciousness. Thus the generation of the universal here is cut off from the manifold of existence—the universal does not emerge out of that manifold. The task now is not so much to purify the individual of his immediate dependency on the senses and to raise him to the substance which thinks and is thought, as it is the reverse, namely, to actualize the universal and to infuse it with spirit by dissolving the fixed determinations of thought. (Ph 30)

This passage teaches us that the speculative and, from Hegel's point of view, positive result of ancient philosophy lies in the purification of the individual from immediate sense knowledge and in his elevation to the universality of thought. It is clear that Hegel is thinking here above all of Plato and Aristotle. And Plato's great accomplishment was in fact that he exposed sense certainty and the belief rooted in it as illusion. He thus made thought so self-sufficient that it might strive to know the truth of reality in the pure universality of thought without interference from sense perception.

In Plato Hegel sees the earliest development of *speculative* dialectic, for Plato goes beyond allowing the universal to emerge indirectly by merely confounding a particular point of view. That the Sophists had done too. In contrast to them, as Hegel sees it, Plato strives to bring the universal into view, purely, by itself, i.e., that which is held to be valid as definition or determination; and that, according to Hegel, means that he seeks to display it in its unity with its opposite. For the very same reason Aristotle is the proper teacher for us all since he is a master at bringing the most various determinations together under one concept. He gathers up all aspects of an idea, as unrelated as he might first find them, while neither leaving determinations out nor seizing first upon one and then upon another; rather, he takes them all together as one. Furthermore, Hegel sees the speculative element in Aristotle in the catholicity of the latter's analysis.

In contrast, the task for modern philosophy, according to Hegel, consists in dissolving fixed, determinate thoughts and thereby actualizing the universal and infusing it with spirit. The meaning of this will concern us subsequently. For now let us accept the point made by Hegel's profound juxtaposition of the ancient and modern, i.e., that ancient philosophy was able to come closer to the fluidity of speculative truth than is possible for modern thought, since the former's concepts had not yet been uprooted from the soil of the concrete plurality of particular existents which they were meant to grasp. They are determinations of thought which have yet to be raised to the universality of self-consciousness, determinations in which "everything that occurs" is thought of in the natural language of natural consciousness. Therefore, ancient dialectic, in Hegel's view, always has the general characteristic of being objective dialectic. If, as is consistent with its meaning, it must be termed negative, it is not negative in the modern sense. Our thinking is not nullified by it, rather the world itself as appearance (cf. XIII, 327). But when ancient philosophy is juxtaposed to modern philosophy, it becomes clear that the mere raising of thought to universality cannot suffice. It remains for the former to discover self-consciousness in this immediately involved universality or "pure certainty of self." According to Hegel the deficiency in the philosophical consciousness of antiquity is that there spirit is still submerged in substance or, put in Hegelian terms, that substance is the concept only "in itself"—that spirit has not yet experienced itself as being "for itself," as subjectivity. Thus it is not conscious of finding itself in its comprehension of what occurs.

Accordingly, ancient dialectic presents these two aspects to Hegel and both, one positive and the other negative, become decisive for his idea of dialectic. That means that his dialectic will need to be "objective." It cannot be a dialectic of our thinking alone, but rather it must also be a dialectic of what is thought, of the concept itself. But it also means that such a dialectic of the concept can only be realized in the development of the concept of the concept, the concept of spirit itself.

If one keeps in view the essential integrity of Hegel's two-sided claim to be both subjective and objective, it becomes clear that the point of Hegelian dialectic is missed not only when one sees in it nothing but a subjective mechanics of thought or as Hegel puts it, a subjective "swing" system of thought: *"raisonnement* going back and forth where there is not content" (Enz 81). It is no less great a mistake to judge Hegel's dialectic in terms of the task which the

Schulmetaphysik of the eighteenth and twentieth centuries set for itself, namely, to grasp the totality of the world in a system of categories. In this case Hegelian dialectic becomes the aimless and fruitless
attempt to construe this system of the world as a universal system of
conceptual relationships.

After Trendelenburg had criticized the beginning of Hegel's *Logic*
for lacking immanent cogency in its resolution of the dialectical contradiction to a higher unity, this second misunderstanding gained
general currency. Trendelenburg believed himself to be noting a deficiency when he pointed out that the dialectical transition from Being
and Nothing to Becoming presupposes a consciousness observing this
movement—as though the movement here were not of self-consciousness thinking itself in all determinations of thought, even those of
Being! Even Dilthey finds Trendelenburg's criticism convincing, and
it constitutes an ultimate barrier for him in his own effort to uncover
what is valuable and enduring in Hegel's dialectic. Dilthey too takes
Hegel's *Logic* to be an attempt to comprehend the world totality in a
system of category-relationships. His criticism of Hegel is directed at
what he considers to be the latter's decisive delusion: that he could
develop the system of logical relationships contained in the entirety
of the world without a foundation such as Fichte still had in the self-
intuition of the ego.[4] As if Hegel, as Rosenkranz relates, had not expressly declared in Jena that the Absolute does not find

> . . . it necessary to give the concept the form of self-consciousness
> right away and to name it "ego," for instance, in order to always
> be reminded of itself in the object of its knowledge. . . . Rather,
> for knowledge, as the unity of universal and individual self-con-
> sciousness, exactly this element and essence is the object and
> content of its science and must for that reason be expressed in
> objective fashion. And thus the object appears as Being. In this,
> as the simple absolute concept, knowledge knows itself imme-
> diately as self-consciousness and therefore it does not occur to
> it that this Being expresses anything opposed to self-conscious-
> ness.[5]

He who misses this point will most certainly view the linear advance
in the dialectical development of concepts as a "dead, endless thread,"

4. Cf. W. Dilthey, *Gesammelte Schriften,* Leipzig and Berlin, 1921, vol. 4,
pp. 226 ff.

5. *Dokumente zu Hegels Entwicklung,* ed. J. Hoffmeister, Stuttgart, 1936.

and to him it will appear proper (when attempting to evaluate Hegel's dialectic positively) to object as did Dilthey and others (J. Cohn, N. Hartmann) that the system of relationships of logical concepts is more various than Hegel saw, that it contains more dimensions, and that Hegel, often forcibly, presses it into the unified line of his own dialectical progression.

This objection might have some justification except that it really is not an objection at all. Hegel does not need to deny, and indeed knows himself, that his exposition does not always penetrate to the necessity of the subject matter itself. He therefore does not shy away from approximating its actual structural divisions in ever different ways, in repeated courses of dialectical development, one alongside the other. Still, Hegel's construction is not an arbitrary one which puts in one line of development that which has no genuine sequentiality at all. For what determine the dialectical development are not the conceptual relationships as such, but rather the fact that in each of these determinations of thought one thinks the "self" of the self-consciousness which claims to state each of these determinations—a "self" whose proper, fully logical exposition comes only at the end, in the "Absolute Idea." The self-movement of the concept, which Hegel's *Logic* attempts to follow, thus rests entirely on the absolute mediation of consciousness and its object, which Hegel thematizes in the *Phenomenology of Mind*. The latter prepares thought for the sphere of pure knowing, which is not at all knowledge of the world totality. For it is not at all knowledge of existent beings in the world, but rather it is always, together with knowledge of what is known, knowledge of knowing. That is the thesis of transcendental philosophy, which Hegel accepts and emphasizes expressly. There is such a thing as the self-movement of the concept only because the object known can never be separated in any way from the knowing subject. That means, though, that the object exists in its truth as an object in the self-consciousness of absolute knowing.

The dialectic of the *Phenomenology of Mind* is similar in this regard. The movement there is a movement in which the distinction between knowing and truth is transcended and at the end of which the total mediation of this distinction emerges in the form of absolute knowing. Nevertheless, for this dialectic too the sphere of pure knowing, of the thinking of self in the thinking of all determinations, is already presupposed. As is well known, Hegel defends himself specifically against the misunderstanding of his *Phenomenology* which takes it to be a propaedeutic introduction not yet having the character of science. The path elevating ordinary consciousness to philosophical consciousness in the course of which the distinction in consciousness, the split between subject and object is eliminated, is, on the contrary, only the *object* of phenomenological science. That science itself is already at the level of science, on which this distinction is transcended. There can be no introduction preceding science. Thinking begins with itself, i.e., with the decision to think.

Thus, whether one is considering the *Logic,* the *Phenomenology,* or any part of speculative science whatsoever, the law governing the movement of this dialectic has its basis in the truth of modern philosophy, the truth of self-consciousness. Simultaneously, however, Hegel's dialectic goes back to ancient dialectic and does so in a more explicit way than would have ever entered the minds of anyone before Hegel, either in the Middle Ages or the modern period. That is already evident in the earliest outlines of his system, the so-called *Jena Logic.* To be sure the dialectical construction there is quite loose. The divisions of the whole still represent the traditional disciplines of philosophy, which are linked in a relatively unconnected way. Hegel's dialectical mastery is better demonstrated here in the particulars of his analysis which, as a whole, does not reach its goal of resolving the tradition to a unified dialectical development. But precisely the incompleteness of the whole makes the historical origin of the material Hegel works through exceptionally clear in its particulars. In *Being and Time* Heidegger points out the connection between Aristotle's *Physics* and the analysis of time in the *Jena Logic* (SZ 432 f.). But beyond this there is even more impressive evidence of the seminal power of dialectic of the Ancients for Hegel—the chapter on the law of identity and contradiction reveals in both its plan and terminology a relationship to Plato's *Parmenides* much closer than is recognizable in the corresponding section of the later *Logic.* In the *Jena Logic* "difference" is even called "the many."[6]

Indeed, the idea of Hegel's *Logic* reflects the fact that in a way the whole of Greek philosophy has been gathered up into his speculative science. Though his point of departure (namely modern philosophy's view that the absolute is life, activity, spirit) may be said to determine his position, it is nevertheless not in the subjectivity of self-consciousness in which he sees the basis of all knowing. Rather, he sees that

6. Hegel, *Jenenser Logik, Metaphysik und Naturphilosophie,* ed. G. Lasson, Hamburg, 1923, pp. 132 ff.

basis in the rational character of all *reality* and, hence, in a concept of spirit as the truly real. This places him squarely within the tradition of Greek *nous*-philosophy, which begins with Parmenides. That is most obvious in the way Hegel develops the most abstract concepts of "Being," "Nothing," and "Becoming"—the first concepts in the history of philosophy—as a homogeneous process in the continuing determination of thought. But it is just as obvious too in the transition he makes from "existence" (*Dasein*) to "that which exists" (*Daseindes*). The law governing this continuing determination is plainly that the simplest and oldest concepts of thought already represent "in themselves" definitions of the Absolute, which is spirit and which therefore reaches fulfillment in the concept of knowing which knows itself. That is the movement of knowing which recognizes itself for the first time in the dialectic of motion with which Greek thought began its course.

That he sees such a movement of self-knowing there is confirmed by a formulation of Hegel's prompted by Zeno's dialectic: "The reason why dialectic first seizes upon motion as its object lies in the fact that dialectic is itself this motion; or, put another way, motion is the dialectic of all that is" (XIII, 313). According to Hegel, the contradiction which Zeno points up in the concept of motion is to be admitted, but nothing is thereby said against motion, but conversely, the reality of contradiction is demonstrated:

> Something moves, not by being here in this "now" and there in another "now"—there where it is at any given time it is not in motion, but at rest—but rather only by being in one and the same "now" here and not here, by being at the same time in this "here" and not in it. (idem)

In the phenomenon of motion, spirit becomes aware of its selfhood for the first time and in immediately intuitive fashion as it were. This occurs because the attempt to speak of motion as something which is, leads to a contradiction. It need not be predicated of what is in motion that it is here and not that it is there—neither is implied in its nature or being. Motion itself is not a predicate of what is moved, not a condition in which some existent being finds itself. Rather it is a very special determination of being. Motion is "the concept of the true soul of the world." "We are accustomed to viewing it as a predicate, as a condition [because our comprehending and speaking of something predicates and thereby fixes], but it is in fact self, subject as subject, the remaining of disappearance" (VII, 64 ff.).

The problem of motion is also behind the later Plato's dialectic to which Hegel devoted particular attention. The petrified tranquility of a cosmos of ideas cannot be the ultimate truth for Plato. For the "soul" which he coordinates with these ideas is motion. Thus, the *logos* which thinks the relationship of the ideas to one another is necessarily a movement of thought and consequently a movement of what is thought. Even though the sense in which motion is supposed to "be" might not be thinkable without contradiction, the dialectic of motion (i.e., the contradiction to which this problem of thinking motion as being leads) cannot keep us from recognizing that motion and being necessarily go together. That is clearly the conclusion reached in the *Sophist* and, seen in this light, the "transition in no time"—that most wondrous nature of the instantaneous of which the *Parmenides* speaks (156 e)—can, in the final analysis, also only be understood to be of positive significance for thought.

But it is in Aristotle's philosophy where the correlation of motion and thought is most basic.[7] Indeed, it is its central theme. Here I would only remind the reader of the way Aristotle's highest speculative concept, *energeia*, expresses this correlation. For Aristotle *energeia* is thinkable only in contrast to *dynamis* and for him *dynamis* has a purely ontological meaning: it no longer means in any sense merely potentiality to move, but rather potentiality to be. Therefore it characterizes the mode of being of that which, if viewed ontologically, is *hylē* (matter). It follows that the corresponding concept of *energeia* also assumes a purely ontological function.[8] It means pure presence (*Anwesenheit*) as such, which in its purity is attributable to the mover, to *nous*, to reason—i.e., to that which properly speaking *is* in the highest sense. The concept of *energeia*, which Aristotle conceives of as pure presence, is without doubt originally a concept of motion and designates the actual carrying out of something as opposed to a mere possibility or capacity. Even if the highest being is entirely without *dynamis*—and that means that there can be no movement in it since all movement implies *dynamis*—there is still plainly discernible in Aristotle's conceptualization of being as *energeia*, something of the nature of that which is in motion. Pure *energeia* transcends the special perpetuity characteristic of the circle and is thought of as

---

7. This relationship is pursued by W. Bröcker in his *Aristoteles*, 2d ed., Frankfurt, 1957.

8. *Metaphysics Eta* and *Theta* are the principal places where Aristotle works out the ontological significance of *dynamis*.

outdoing it, as it were.[9] Only because that is so can Aristotle believe, as it clearly seems he does, that in his determination of motion he has gotten beyond the mere dialectical juxtaposition of being and not-being, and that he has left Plato behind him in defining the nature of motion as the "*energeia* of the possible as possible."

How much the dialectic of motion, which so dominates Plato's and Aristotles' philosophy, coincided with Hegel's interest will become even clearer subsequently when we examine his appropriation of Greek philosophy more closely. Let it suffice to say here that he saw in it the "absolute tendency of all education and philosophy" towards the determination of the Absolute as spirit. The problem which motion poses for thought is that of continuity, of the *syneches*. The task which Hegel sets for himself turns on this problem. That is demonstrated by his belief in the homogeneity of the dialectical procedure, in which the relationship of thought and motion is "reflected." But even in those cases where the attempt has been made to evade the absolute mediation of Hegel's dialectic, the problem of motion characteristically persists as such, e.g., in Trendelenburg's logical investigations, in Herman Cohen's concept of the source (*Ursprung*), in Dilthey's avowals of his ever greater recognition of Hegel's accomplishments, in Husserl's doctrine of intentionality and of the stream of consciousness (specifically in his extension of this doctrine into one of horizon intentionality and "anonymous" intentionality) and, finally, in Heidegger's discovery of the fundamental role time plays in ontology.

In view of the congruity existing between the dialectic of motion and the dialectic of thought, Hegel's use of Greek philosophy seems well justified. But there now arises the question of how Hegel's own understanding of the opposition between ancient and modern times and of the difference in the problem posed for thought then and for his thought is expressed in the use he makes of ancient dialectic. Through dialectic Hegel claims to have made fluid the rigid categories of the Understanding. Modern thought had gotten caught in the self-contradictions of these categories. But dialectic, he says, makes it possible to transcend the Understanding's distinction between subject and substance and to recognize both the form of self-consciousness immersed in substance and the form of its pure inwardness by

9. One must always view Aristotle's teachings on pure *energeia* against the background of the theory of modes of movement in Plato's *Laws* X (893b–899). Cf. above all, 898a. See "Über das Göttliche ..." in my *Kleine Schriften* III, Mohr, 1967.

itself, as two false forms of one and the same movement of spirit. To describe how the traditional ontological categories of the Understanding become fluid, Hegel uses a specific characterization: "They infuse themselves with spirit (*sich begeisten*)." Specifically, that means that they are no longer meant to grasp reality in opposition to self-consciousness, but rather to grasp spirit as the truth proper to modern philosophy. Originally, as Greek terms, these concepts were intended to express the being of nature, of what is present around us; and they broke into dialectical oppositions when they ran up against the movement of everything in nature. But now their self-negation, their reduction to self-contradiction is supposed to bring forth the higher truth of spirit. Since it is in the nature of spirit to sustain contradiction and to maintain itself precisely therein as the speculative unity of things opposed to each other, contradiction, which was proof of worthlessness for the Ancients, becomes something positive for modern philosophy. The nullity of what is merely there around us, of that which is said to exist in the "real" world, brings forth the higher truth of "what is the subject or the concept."

There is, however, absolutely nothing of this in the dialectic of the Ancients. Even Plato's *Parmenides* is presented as an exercise without result. Given this state of affairs, how is it to be explained that Hegel thought himself to be reviving classical dialectic? Even if the dialectic of motion really does correspond to the dialectic of spirit, how can Hegel believe that the negative dialectic of motion which was worked out by Zeno and then repeated by Plato on a higher level of reflection, provides the methodological model for his own dialectical method? How are their efforts, which lead to nothing, supposed to demonstrate the ultimate truth that the absolute is spirit?

In order to resolve this question we must focus on Hegel's own testimony regarding his dialectical method. We must make our point of departure Hegel's questioning of the statement as a proper vehicle for expression of the speculative essence of philosophy. For before all consideration of the logic of speculative philosophy, he says, must come the realization that the form of the statement or judgment respectively is inappropriate for the expression of speculative truths (cf. Enz 61–62). Philosophy demands comprehension. But the structure of the statement, of the ordinary judgment of the Understanding, it is argued, cannot satisfy this demand.

Underlying the usual judgment is a subject (*hypokeimenon-subjectum*) and the content, the predicate, is related to the latter as its *accidens.* The movement of determination runs back and forth across this posited existent, i.e., the subject, which is taken as a fixed basis. The subject can be determined as this or that, in one respect in one way, in another respect in another way. The respects in which the subject is judged are external to the subject itself which means that it always can be judged in still other respects. Determination here is thus external to the subject matter and accordingly there is no necessity at all in its development: for the fixed subject-basis of all these determinations extends beyond everything which is ascribed to it, since, in fact, additional predicates can also be ascribed to it. All such determinations are thus gathered extrinsically and stand alongside of each other in a purely external relationship. Even when the ideal of a conclusive proof seems to be realized within the context of a self-enclosed deduction, e.g., in mathematical knowing, Hegel still sees the same externality (cf. *Ph,* "Preface"). For the auxiliary constructions which make a geometrical proof possible, for example, are not deduced necessarily from the subject matter itself. They first have to occur to us even if their validity is eventually made evident by the proof.

With polemic acridity Hegel terms all such judgments of the Understanding *raisonnement.* To begin with, *raisonnement* has a negative connotation which is still evident today in the meaning of the German *raisonnieren.* In *raisonnieren* knowledge of the subject matter is not really advanced by the negative insight that something "isn't so," for the positive moment which lies in every negation does not become the new content of the observations being made. On the contrary, *raisonnieren* gets caught up in its vain negativity and is reflected into itself. It is content to make judgments about the subject matter and in so doing does not stay with it, but rather has already moved on to something else: "Instead of dwelling on it and losing itself in it, such knowing always grasps for something else. Thus it remains by itself rather than being with the subject matter and yielding to it" (Ph 11). More importantly, though, so-called "positive" knowledge of something is *raisonnement* too in the sense that it makes a subject basic and proceeds from one idea to another relating each of these ideas to this subject. It is characteristic of both the negative and positive forms of *raisonnieren* that the movement of such apprehension in thought runs its course externally upon the surface of the thing as if the latter were unmoved and inert.

In contrast to *raisonnement,* speculative thinking comprehends (*begreift*). The natural tendency of determination to reach out beyond the subject of the sentence to other things in terms of which the subject matter is determined as "this" or "that," is blocked. "It experiences a counter-impetus, as it were. It starts with the subject, as if this remained lying at the base of the matter, but since, on the contrary, the predicate is the substance *[subjectum]*, it discovers that the subject has passed over into the predicate and is thereby sublimated. And since that which seemed to be a predicate thus becomes a complete, independent mass, thought is not free to wander errantly, rather it is arrested by this weight" (Ph 50). The movement of comprehending (*begreifendes*) thought which Hegel describes with this and a series of other metaphors, he characterizes as something unaccustomed. It places a great demand upon "representative" thought's way of relating to things. By nature we want to learn something new about the thing, and accordingly we reach out beyond the foundation of the subject to something else which we ascribe to it as a predicate. But philosophic statements are quite a different matter. Here there is no firm foundation, no subject which, as such, remains unquestioned. Here our thought does not come to a predicate which refers to something else, but rather to a predicate which forces us to go back to the subject. We do not take up something new or different in the predicate, for in thinking the predicate, we are actually penetrating into that which the subject is. The *subjectum* taken as a firm foundation is abandoned, since thought does not think something else in the predicate but rather rediscovers the subject itself. Hence, to ordinary, "representative" thinking a philosophical statement is always something like a tautology: the philosophical statement expresses an identity. In it the supposed difference between subject and predicate is transcended. Properly speaking the philosophical statement is no longer a statement at all. Nothing is posited in it which is supposed to remain, for the "is" or copula of the statement has an entirely different function here. It does not state the being of something using something else, but rather describes the movement in which thought passes over from the subject into the predicate in order to find there the firm ground which it has lost.

In one instance Hegel clarifies this movement using the example, "The real is the universal." This statement not only asserts that the real is universal: here the universal is further meant to express the essence of the real. Insofar as the concept of the real is more precisely defined in this statement, thought cannot be said to be passing beyond that concept. Indeed, the real is not determined as something other than itself, but rather as that which it is. Since it proves to be the universal, the universal is the true subject of thought. The consequence is, however, that thought goes back into itself. Thought's reflection here is reflection into self since in fact it does not reflect *about* something while going outside of its content in order to bring in other determinations of reflection, but rather immerses itself in its own content, i.e., in that which the subject itself is. That, according to Hegel, is the essence of dialectical speculation—thinking nothing other than this selfhood, thinking the being of self itself, in which the ego of self-consciousness has always already recognized itself. Accordingly, the subjectivity of self-consciousness is the subject of all statements, whose predicates are the simple abstractions or determinations of thinking as they are thought purely by themselves.

Philosophical speculation thus begins with the "decision to try to think purely" (Enz 102). Thinking purely means thinking only that which is being thought of and nothing else. Thus, as Hegel says on one occasion, speculation is the pure observation of that alone which can be called valid determination. To think of a determination is not to think of something else to which the determination belongs, i.e., something else which is not the determination itself. Rather, the determination is to be thought "in itself": it is to be determined as that which it is. But accordingly, it in itself is both what is determined and what does the determining. In that the determination relates itself to itself, that which is determined is at the same time another to itself. At this point, however, it has already been pushed to the contradiction lying within itself, and it now finds itself in the movement of its sublimation, that is, it produces for itself the "simple unity" of that which had split apart in the opposition of identity on the one hand and nonidentity as the negation of itself on the other. In a given determination, "pure thinking" thinks nothing other than this determination itself and in so doing it thinks nothing adventitious such as the faculty of representation (*Vorstellung*) is wont to imagine (*vorzustellen*). It thus discovers in itself the origin of all further determination. Only when the completed mediation of all determinations, the identity of identity and nonidentity, is thought of in the concept of the concept or in spirit, respectively, can the movement of progression into the self come to rest. Hegel, therefore, terms the speculative movement immanently formative, which is to say that it continues to form itself out of itself. Opposed to this is what "occurs" to one, i.e., the importation of notions which are not inherent in a determination, but rather which it "brings to mind" and which in thus occurring to

one interrupt and disturb the immanent course of such ongoing self-
formation of the concepts.[10] Hegel finds that just as subjective thinking, to which something "occurs," is diverted from the direction of
what it had been thinking by what "comes to mind," our penetration
into the concept as it continues to determine itself is diverted by notions or intrusions of external imagination. In philosophy no notions
are good. For every notion is a transition to something else without
connection, a transition lacking necessity and insight. But according
to Hegel, philosophy should be the necessary, evident, "homogeneous
(*gediegener*)" progress of the concept itself.

This formal characteristic of the continuing determination of
thought in itself does not necessitate that it be proven ahead of time
that the contradictions themselves which emerge will unify themselves
by fusing into a new *positum*, into a new simple self. Properly speaking, the new content is not deduced, but always has proven itself already to be that which endures the severity of contradiction and
maintains itself as one therein, namely, the self of thought.

In short, there are three elements which, according to Hegel, may
be said to be essential to dialectic. First, thinking is thinking of something in itself taken by itself. Second, as such it necessarily thinks
contradictory determinations simultaneously. Third, the unity of
contradictory determinations has, in that these are sublimated in that
unity, the proper nature of the self. Hegel is of the opinion that all
three of these elements are to be found in the dialectic of the Ancients.

Turning to the first point, we see that even in the earliest dialectic
such thinking of determinations by themselves is clearly evident. Only
the decision to try to think purely and to avoid imaginative notions
could have led to the incredibly daring thought characteristic of Eleatic philosophy. And indeed we find that even Zeno, with the fullest
awareness of what he is doing, employs such thought, for example,
in the first three fragments in Diels's collection, which are taken from
Simplicius. Zeno's demonstration—that if there were "a many" it
would have to be infinitely small because it would consist of the
smallest parts without size, and at the same time it would have to be
infinitely large since it would consist of infinitely many such parts—

---

10. There would appear to be little disagreement now that Baillie's translation of *Begriff* as "notion" was misleading. As Gadamer points out here Hegel
distinguishes sharply between what is a mere notion (*Einfall, Vorstellung*) and
what is a true concept (*Begriff*). (TRANS.)

rests on the presupposition that both determinations, that of the smallness and that of the multiplicity of the parts, are thought by themselves, and in each case lead by themselves to determinations of the "many." The second element too, i.e., simultaneous thinking of contradictory determinations, is present in the argument here, to the extent that the argument is intended as an indirect refutation of the hypothesis of the "many." But it is such a refutation only insofar as smallness and size are to be directly ascribed to the many and not in different respects. A separation of the different aspects of multiplicity and smallness would, in fact, prevent the contradiction. The form of the argument corresponds exactly to the one which the Ancients attributed to the "Eleatic Palamedes"[11]: the contradiction of every statement must be investigated along with the statement itself and the consequences of both developed. To be sure, in Zeno the point of thinking determinations together and by themselves is a negatively dialectical one. That which is determined by such contradiction is, as contradictory, null and void. Thus the third element of Hegelian dialectic which we singled out, namely, the positive content of contradiction, is missing here.

But this, too, Hegel believes he is able to find in ancient dialectic, though not before Plato. Hegel agrees, of course, that dialectic in Plato often has only the negative purpose of confounding preconceptions. As such it is only a subjective variation of Zeno's dialectic. By the use of external conceptions, it is able to refute every assertion—a technique cultivated particularly by the Sophists and pursued without positive results. But aside from this Hegel sees in Plato a positive, speculative dialectic, one that leads to objective contradictions, but not merely in order to nullify their presuppositions. Plato's speculative dialectic also contains an insight into the contradiction and antithesis of being and not-being, on the one hand, and of difference and non-difference, on the other. Implied, Hegel maintains, is that Plato recognized that these belong together and hence entail a higher unity. For this interpretation Hegel relies above all on Plato's *Parmenides*, his understanding of it being shaped in large part by Neoplatonism's theological-ontological interpretation of the latter. There, in what very much seems to be a radicalization of Zeno's dialectic, the conversion of one postulation into its opposite is demonstrated—and, to be sure, in a process of mediation in which each of these determina-

11. Palamedes was a famous wrestler whose name was often used, as in this case, to refer to Zeno. (TRANS.)

tions is thought of abstractly by itself. (Of course, Hegel, in reference
to the dialectic in the *Parmenides*, inserts the qualification, as we have
already mentioned, that it is not yet pure dialectic, but rather one
which begins with given conceptions, e.g., the statement, "The one
is." But if one allows this nonnecessary beginning, then, says Hegel,
this dialectic is "entirely proper.")

Still, in Plato's works the *Parmenides* has a character all its own.
To say the least, it is problematic whether pointing up contradictions
as the *Parmenides* does could have a positive demonstrative purpose or
whether it is not merely a propaedeutic exercise meant to dissolve the
inflexible thesis of the ideas and the rigid Eleatic concept of reality
underlying it. But, whatever the case in the *Parmenides*, Hegel now
proceeds to read Plato's *Sophist* assuming that the dialectic there has
the same sense as that he saw in the *Parmenides*, and on the basis of
this assumption he concludes that in the *Sophist* it is in fact asserted
that absolute contradictions have positive content. Decisive here, as
he sees it, is that Plato contends that the identical must be recognized
in one and the same respect as different. As has long been established,
Hegel arrives at this view through a total misunderstanding of passage
259b in the *Sophist*.[12] His translation reads, "What is difficult to
grasp yet true is that what is another is the same, and *specifically in
one and the same regard,* in reference to the *same* aspect" (XIV 233).
What is actually said is that what is difficult to grasp yet true is that
when someone says, the same is in some way different, one must in-
quire in *which* sense and in *which* respect it is different. Taking the
same as different in a vague sense without specification of the respect
and producing contradictions in this way is, contrary to Hegel's interpretation, expressly characterized as purposeless and as a concern of
beginners only.

There can be no doubt that the particular reference here and, in
fact, the reference to the *Sophist* as a whole as an example of "Eleatic" but nevertheless "positive" dialectic is unjustified. Plato sees
the essence of his doctrine of the *logos* and the fundamental difference of this doctrine from that of Eleatic philosophy in the fact that
he progresses beyond the abstract opposition of being and nonbeing
to the possibility of their noncontradictory unification in the determinations of reflection, identity, and difference. This insight provides
a positive justification for the business of the dialectician, namely dif-

---

12, K. L. W. Heyder, *Kritische Darstellung der Aristotelischen und Hegelschen Dialektik,* Erlangen, 1845.

ferentiation, classification, definition—in spite of the apparent contradiction in saying that the same is one and many. There is no mention here of pushing a hypothesis to self-contradiction nor, moreover, is there any mention of the emergence of a higher self in which abstract determinations, which, if thought by themselves, are contradictory and require sublimation, are resolved to the simple unity of a synthesis. On the contrary, sameness and difference are illustrated by showing that a thing standing in relationship to something else is at the same time different in one respect and the same in another. Thus, the point of the *Sophist* accords very little with Hegel's intent, namely to establish in the place of so-called formal logic the dialectic of contradiction as the method of the higher, speculative logic. Rather, one finds in the *Sophist* (230 b) a first formulation of formal logic's law of noncontradiction as set up by Aristotle in book IV of his *Metaphysics*.

Plato plainly wants to keep true division and determination separate from the eristic art of false dialectic. It may be that what he has in mind contains the *aporia* of the one and the many within it, but the specific purpose of the *Sophist* is to break the spell of falsity cast in speaking and argument when, without specification of the respect, one demonstrates something to be both the same and different.

To begin with, let us ask ourselves what Hegel's misinterpretation of this passage in Plato implies, i.e., what positive view in this matter Hegel has which makes him convert the meaning of a not particularly obscure passage into its opposite. One who is familiar with Hegel will understand why Hegel refuses to listen when Plato stipulates there that in every case the respect must be specified in which something is identical or different. For such a requirement directly contradicts Hegel's dialectical method. The latter, namely, consists in thinking a determination in itself and by itself, so that it displays its onesidedness and thus forces us to think its opposite. The opposed determinations are pushed to contradiction precisely by being thought *in abstracto*, by themselves. Hegel sees the speculative nature of reflection here: what stands in contradiction is reduced to *momenta*, the unity of which is the truth. In opposition to this approach, he argues, the Understanding strives to avoid contradictions and, where it encounters an antithesis, to restrict it as best it can to mere, insignificant differentness. To be sure, what is different is seen in a common respect, namely that of dissimilarity (which always implies a respect in which there is similarity). But in differentiating one does not reflect on this. Differentiation considers only different aspects of the thing in which the latter's similarity and dissimilarity are evident. According to Hegel, the Understanding attempts to fix thought at this standpoint. It removes the unity of similarity and dissimilarity from the thing and transfers it to thought per se, which thinks both in its operations.[13]

In both cases, that of similarity and of dissimilarity, the Understanding avails itself of the same means to avoid thinking the determinations in themselves, i.e., thinking their pure conceptual content. It strives not to think of them *qua* subject, but rather as predicates attributed to a subject and which accordingly can be attributed to it in different regards. As a result, abstract determinations stand alongside each other in an indifferent "too," since they are not thought of as determinations as such, but rather as the attributes of something else. "Using the devices of 'insofar as' and 'in this respect,' the Understanding struggles against bringing /the determinations/ together and thereby sublimating them. Or it assumes responsibility itself for one thought in order to preserve the other as true" (Ph 102). Precisely that which Plato advances against the Sophists as the precondition of philosophical thought, Hegel calls the sophistry of the Understanding and representative thought. Must we not conclude that Hegel's own procedure, which leaves the respects unspecified in order to push determinations to contradiction, would be called sophistic by Plato and Aristotle?

But still, even if he is mistaken about specifics, has Hegel not understood Plato's position as a whole correctly? Is he not correct in seeing the dialectic of the determinations of reflection, i.e., identity and difference, in the *Sophist*? Was it not Plato's great accomplishment to have elevated the abstract Eleatic opposition of being and nonbeing to the speculative relationship of "is" and "is not," the content of which are the determinations of reflection, identity, and difference? And beyond that, is Hegel's interpretation not justified since the task which he sets for himself, namely that of making fixed determinations of thought fluid, converges with Plato's insight into the inevitable bewilderment which results from all utterances? Plato speaks of the inescapable *pathos tōn logōn* as if entanglement in contradiction were the lot of thought. Plato too sees that not only as negative. On the contrary, he sees in Socrates a new possibility be-

13. As is common knowledge, Hegel's criticism of Kant's transcendental dialectic is that Kant, out of "tenderness for the things," ascribes the contradiction to the Understanding. Cf. XV 582.

yond the confusion which was introduced into all established concepts and viewpoints when the Greek Enlightenment's rhetoric and mode of argument degenerated into a form of demonic possession. The power of talk to perplex can have a genuine philosophic function: by confounding preconceptions, it is capable of opening up a view of the true relationships of things. Plato's own account of philosophical knowing in *Epistle VII* makes it clear that the positive and negative functions of *logos* both derive from the nature of the matter.[14] The "means" of knowing (i.e., the word, the concept, the intuition or picture, the opinion or point of view, without which any use of *logos* is impossible) are in themselves ambiguous since each of them can assert itself and in so doing display itself instead of the thing intended. It lies in the character of the statement that it itself does not insure proper understanding of its meaning. On the contrary, it can always be understood falsely, i.e., too literally. That is of no mean significance, for we see that the very thing which makes possible a vision of things as they are can distort them at the same time. Philosophy cannot be distinguished from sophistic *raisonnement* if attention is paid only to what is stated as such.[15] Knowledge of the truth can only be attained in the reality of live discussion, in which "men of good will and genuine dedication to the subject matter" reach agreement with each other. Thus all philosophy remains dialectic, for all utterances, even those, indeed precisely those which express the inner structure and differentiation of the subject matter, i.e., the relationship of the ideas to each other, carry within themselves the contradiction of the "one" and the "many" and thus also lend themselves to eristic exploitation of that same contradiction.

In fact, as the *Parmenides* demonstrates, Plato himself is capable of something similar to such eristic exploitation. What appeared to be the one truth of Socratic dialectic—the indestructible constancy of single idea, which alone seems to guarantee the unity of what is

14. *Epist. VII,* 341–43. [See also Gadamer's "Dialektik und Sophistik im Siebenten Platonischen Brief," in *Platos Dialektische Ethik,* pp. 223 ff. (TRANS.)]

15. To be sure, the *Sophist,* a dialogue which is concerned with how things can be discriminated from each other, does succeed in explaining how such a thing as a sophist is possible. And in the process an ontological understanding of appearance or the being of nonbeing is reached. But differentness as such, in terms of which Plato comprehends sophistic apparent truths, is also basic to the truth of philosophy. How the true *logos* is to be distinguished from the false is obviously not evident in the *logos* itself.

meant—is here not just simply true with qualification. In Plato's in-
geniously devised confrontation, the elder Parmenides makes the
young Socrates see clearly enough that the latter had attempted to define the idea too soon and that he must now learn to dissolve the fixed
idea taken as unrelated to anything else.[16] Every utterance is by nature
just as much a one as it is a many because reality is differentiated in itself. It itself is *logos.*

One may gain quite precise insight about the nature of predication
and as a result one may be very successful in combatting the Sophistic
rhetorical art of bewildering people. Still, in the properly philosophical
realm where the essential is stated—e.g., in definition—we are not dealing with predication, but rather with the speculative self-differentiation
of the essence. The *logos ousias,* according to its structure, is a speculative statement in which the so-called predicate is actually the subject.
Quite apart from the eristic art of misusing the contradiction of unity
and multiplicity for argument's sake—something termed childish by
Plato—there is hidden in the speculative utterance an *aporia* which is
to be taken seriously. It is the irresolvable contradiction of the one
and the many which, in spite of the problem it confronts us with, is
a rich source of advancement in our knowledge of things.[17] What is
hinted at in the *Philebos* is confirmed in the *Sophist,* where the exposition of the dialectic of the species remains itself basically "dialectical." Once the dialectical correlation of "difference" itself with
"sameness" itself, of notbeing with being, has been asserted, there
can be no simple characterization of the respect in which something
is different. A philosophic statement, which in division of the ideas
undertakes to determine the nature of things, specifically presupposes
the speculative relationship of unity in what is opposite. To this extent Hegel is not completely unjustified in seeking support for his
views in Plato.

It is logical, then, that Hegel would emphasize Plato's claim that
his dialectic of ideas surpasses the necessity in mathematics. In the
former there is no need of figures, i.e., of imported constructions
adduced prior to the proof—which for its part is also extrinsic. Rather, the course of thought proceeds, as Plato puts it in book VI of the
Republic, strictly from idea to idea without bringing in anything at
all from outside. As is well known, Plato sees the answer to the problem he poses for thought in *diairesis*—the division of the subject mat-

16. *Parmenides* 135c.
17. *Philebus* 15bc.

ter under consideration which evolves according to the structure of that subject matter, i.e., according to the logical differences lying within it. Thus Hegel sharply disagrees with Aristotle, who finds this method of concept classification lacking in logical rigor and who therefore distinguishes dialectic from valid demonstration.[18] For Hegel, in contrast, not the ideal of logical cogency but that of philosophical demonstration is paramount, i.e., the immanent, continuing explication of thought. And that is something very much closer to the step by step division and definition of Plato's dialogue. There is no deduction here, rather an exchange of question and answer through which an understanding of the subject matter is reached. As a matter of fact, Aristotle's logical criticism does not apply to Plato's dialogues. Only where Plato, in imitation of Parmenides and Zeno, tries his hand at monological dialectic is the unity of immanent development, or "tangling" as Hegel puts it, lacking.

In turning to Hegel's appropriation of Aristotle's philosophy, we see that understanding and misunderstanding are mixed in equal measure. From what has been said it is evident that the logic proper to the dialectical method cannot be derived from Aristotle in any way. On the contrary, it is a highly paradoxical twist that Hegel ranks Aristotle's catholic *empeiria* as "speculative." On the other hand, the quote from Aristotle (*Meta.* XII 7) with which Hegel concludes the exposition of his system in the *Encyclopedia* (Enz 463) demonstrates how much of his own views he was able to find in the content of Aristotle's philosophy.

A closer examination of his interpretation of this passage in his *Lectures on the History of Philosophy* is quite instructive in this regard. That interpretation is to be found in two places: XIV, 330 ff. and (in reference to *De anima* III, 4) on pp. 390 ff. It cannot be disputed that in the passage in question Aristotle is setting forth the truly speculative identity of the subjective and objective as the culmination of his metaphysics. But Hegel also sees clearly that in spite of this Aristotle does not give this identity the principal systematic function which it has for speculative idealism:

> For Aristotle, thinking is an object like any other—a kind of condition. He does not say that it alone is the truth, or that every thing is thought. Rather he says that it is the primary, mightiest, and most esteemed thing. It is we who say that thought as that which relates itself to itself *is*, is the truth. Further, we say that

18. *Analyt. Pr.* I, 31.

thought is *all* truth, but not Aristotle. . . . Aristotle does not express himself as philosophy now speaks, but the same point of
view is basic to him. (idem)

Let us see whether in fact it is. Without doubt the concern here is
a matter of nuances in interpretation of the Aristotelian texts. Still it
is not just a question of how one might choose to read these texts.
Rather, if one departs from the passage taken by Hegel, one can spot
the almost imperceptible shifts in meaning which he in fact makes in
interpreting Aristotle's thought. Hegel's account of how Aristotle derives his conception of the highest *nous* from the same idea as Hegel's
is entirely correct: *nous* thinks itself "in taking what is thought as its
object. Thus it is receptive. However, it *is* being thought in that it also
affects and thinks. Thus the thought and what is thought are the same."
Hegel's interpretation of that is that "the object converts into activity,
energeia." Undoubtedly Aristotle intends something else though,
namely, the reverse: thought becomes an "object," i.e., what is
thought. Moreover, Hegel believes that his idea of the conversion into
energeia is further substantiated when he finds Aristotle saying, "For
that which takes up the thing thought and the essence, is the thought."
More explicit is the passage on p. 390: "Its taking up is activity and it
produces that which appears as that being taken up—it is active in that
it has."[19] Thus, Hegel thinks even of receptivity or taking up as activity. But that too is erroneous. To be sure, Aristotle means without
doubt that that which can receive already has the character of thought,
but this thinking is only actual when it has received, and he concludes
from this that acting and not potentiality is the divine element in
thought. This conclusion is to be found substantially in Hegel's para-
phrasing, but not as a conclusion he reaches. On the contrary, for
Hegel the *presupposition* of the priority of effectivity is so self-evident
that he no longer recognizes at all that the analysis of the connection
between being able to take up a thought and having it is, in Aristotle's
considerations, meant to justify a subsequent conclusion. Thus the
result Hegel arrives at is certainly correct: "*nous* only thinks itself because it is most excellent" (391). But for Hegel this statement obviously means that the self of thought, free activity, is highest and not,
on the other hand, something that is thought. For Aristotle, however,
the determination of what is highest must start directly with what is

19. In the text there is either an editor's or printer's mistake: "er wird" instead of "er wirkt." Cf. p. 331, "Es wirkt, sofern es hat," and the continuation
of this thought on p. 390, "das Ganze des Wirkens . . . das Wirkendste."

thought. He concludes as follows: if *nous* is to be the highest, as has now been established, that which it thinks, the thing thought, may not be anything other than itself. Therefore it thinks itself.[20]

This ordering of things corresponds to Plato's line of thought in the *Sophist*. The movement of being known and being thought is first attributed to reality or being and then, only subsequently, is it said that reality or being must involve life and the movement of intelligence.[21] There too it seems most logical to start with being thought and not primarily with the self thinking itself. That implies, however, that the self thinking itself, which is on the same level as soul, life, and movement, cannot be taken as "activity." *Energeia,* being at work, is not intended to characterize a generative source in the free spontaneity of the self but rather the unlimited, full being of the creative process, which fulfills itself in what is created, the *ergon.* Thus, in a manner of speaking, Hegel explicates the Greek form of "reflection into self" starting at the wrong end, namely with that which Hegel himself praises as the actual discovery of modern philosophy—that the absolute is activity, life, spirit.

The modification of the original meaning of the Greek text is not as palpable in Hegel's interpretation of Aristotle as it was in his interpretation of the passage from Plato treated above. The basic reason for this is that the concept of "life," which is fundamental to Greek thinking about reality, also plays a fundamental role in Hegel's attempt to distance himself critically from the subjectivity of modern philosophy. An irreconcilable difference remains, however, inasmuch as Hegel, relying on his conception of spirit, i.e., recognition of self in the other, defines life as "reflection into self." The Greeks, in contrast, think of that which moves itself or that which has the origin of motion in itself, as primary. Starting from there, i.e., from what is

20. The painstaking analysis of Hegel's translation of *De anima* III, 4–5 published by Walter Kern in *Hegel-Studien* 1, Bonn, 1961 (pp. 49 ff.) serves very nicely to establish the direction in which Hegel's understanding of Aristotle tends, and it complements my exposition above. Still, I find it hard to believe that it is only in the late phases of Hegel's interpretation of Aristotle where the systematic consequences of absolute idealism become evident. For that reason, I would prefer to speak, not so much of a misunderstanding on Hegel's part, as of a progressive understanding which always and necessarily implies a process of building what is understood into his own thought. (That would not only hold for Hegel.)

21. *Sophist* 248d ff. Cf. "Über das Göttliche" in my *Kleine Schriften* III.

encountered in the world, they carry over the structure of self-referentiality into their conception of *nous.*

A particularly illuminating text which points up this difference is *De anima* III, 6, 430b, 20 ff. Indeed, the opposition in living things of *steresis* and *eidos* is here translated into an explanation of the relationship between knower and what is known.[22] Where there is no *steresis,* thinking thinks itself or, in other words, there exists the pure self-presentation of the *eidos.* Thus it is the self-referentiality of reality, what is thought, which gives thought the characteristic of thinking itself, not a self-referential thinking which as such would be the highest reality. In this regard too the meaning of things is changed in Hegel's interpretation. The priorities in Aristotle's train of thought are unmistakable: the self-differentiation of things is primary, the differentiation which thought carries out, secondary. Differentiation which thought makes within itself so that it "thinks itself" is yet a third matter, which follows necessarily from the line of argument being developed. Accordingly, it is only in the result where Aristotle and Hegel converge—the structure of self-referentiality as such.

But let us return from these convergences and divergences which exist between Hegel and Greek philosophy, to what is properly speaking a logical consideration—i.e., how can Hegel proceed to exalt dialectic by making it the very form of philosophical demonstration? We are now in a position to see that the Greek model, in spite of any reliance of Hegel's on Eleatic and Platonic dialectic, is of no help to us here. What Hegel correctly sees in the Greeks is that which he sees everywhere where philosophy exists—speculation. Philosophic statements cannot be understood as judgments in the sense of predicative logic. That is not only valid for expressly "dialectical" thinkers like Heracleitus or Plato. As Hegel correctly sees, it is valid for Aristotle too, even though it is he who explains the structure of predication by uncovering its logical form as well as its ontological basis and who, in so doing, breaks the spell cast by the Sophists' rhetorical techniques.

What is it that allows Hegel to discern the speculative element in Aristotle with such accuracy? Is it because the power of Hegel's thought allows him to penetrate the rigidified language of *die Schulmetaphysik,* allows him in interpreting Aristotle to follow the traces of the speculative wherever they might appear? We know much better

---

22. The relationship of *steresis* and *eidos* in Aristotle's thought is pursued by Gadamer in the "epilogue" to his translation of *Metaphysics* XII, Frankfurt, 1948, pp. 46 ff. (TRANS.)

today how great Hegel's achievement is. For we are on the verge of being able to explain the concepts which Aristotle arrives at as the product of the language-instinct which he thought follows.[23]

Thus we have come full circle in our observations for this was precisely the point where Hegel, determined as he was by modern circumstances, found his own philosophical endeavor confronted with a problem precisely the opposite of that which the Ancients faced. His concern was to "make fluid" the fixed suppositions of the Understanding, "to infuse them with spirit." Hegel's aim of restoring the philosophic demonstration derives from his desire to dissolve in spirit's being at home with itself everything "positive," everything estranged and alien.

Two things serve Hegel in accomplishing his task: first, the dialectical method of radicalizing a position until it becomes self-contradictory and, second, his ability to conjure up the speculative content hidden in the logical instinct of language. In both regards ancient philosophy was helpful to him. He worked out his own dialectical method by extending the dialectic of the Ancients and transforming it into a sublimation of contradiction into ever higher syntheses. We saw that his reliance here upon the Greeks is justified only in part, i.e., in reference to the content, but not to the method. But for the other side of his undertaking, for the guidance in speculation which the logical instinct of language is able to provide, ancient philosophy was paradigmatic. Though in no sense a linguistic purist, Hegel, in seeking to overcome the estranged language of *die Schulmetaphysik*, in suffusing its foreign phrases and artificial expressions with the concepts of ordinary thought, succeeded in recovering the speculative spirit of his native tongue for the speculative movement of his philosophizing, and thereby restored a way of doing philosophy which is the natural inheritance from the first Greek thinkers. Hegel's methodological principle—the requirement of an immanently developing progression in which concepts move to ever greater differentiation and concretization—thus remains grounded in the logical instinct of language and the guidance which it provides. The form in which philosophy is presented can, as Hegel himself admits, never be entirely divorced from the form of the statement and thus must maintain the appearance of a predicative structure.

Here it even seems proper to me to go beyond Hegel's understand-

23. Compare the work of Ernst Kapp, Bruno Snell, Günter Patzig, Wolfgang Wieland.

ing of himself and to acknowledge that the dialectical development of
thought and listening to the speculative spirit in one's own language
are in the final analysis of the same nature. They themselves exist in
dialectical unity, i.e., in indissoluble correlation with each other. For
the speculative is only actual when it is not solely retained inwardly
in mere opinion, but rather when it is also expressed, be this in the
form of explicit philosophic exposition, in contradiction and its resolution, or in the covert tensions within the spirit of language prevailing
over us. When Hegel analyzes the speculative statement in the preface
to him *Phenomenology,* he makes clear what the role is of expression
and express presentation in the form of dialectical radicalization of
the subject matter, and he thus establishes the importance of such
expression and presentation for his idea of philosophic demonstration.
It is not only that "natural consciousness" is thus placated by having
the speculative element in its thought pointed out to it. Hegel is here
meeting the demands of the Understanding and when he goes that far
a principle is at stake which Hegel is asserting generally against modern
subjectivity and the latter's preference for the inner realm—"The un-
derstandable is what is already known and held in common by science
and the unscientific consciousness." Hegel sees the untruth of pure
inwardness not only in such withering forms of consciousness as the
"beautiful soul" and the man of "good will." He sees it in all previous
forms of philosophic speculation, insofar as these do not express the
contradictions which the speculative unity of philosophic concepts
contains.

Plainly, the concepts of exposition and expression, which properly
define the essence of dialectic, the *reality* of the speculative, must, like
Spinoza's *exprimere,* be understood as referring to an ontological process. "Exposition," "expression," being stated, demarcate a conceptual
field behind which lies the grand tradition of Neoplatonism. "Expression" is not a matter of subjective choice, i.e., something added on after
after the fact and by virtue of which the meaning in the private sphere
is made communicable. Rather it is the coming into existence of spirit
itself, its "exposition." The Neoplatonic origin of these concepts is not
accidental. The determinations within which thought moves are, as
Hegel emphasizes, not extrinsic forms which we apply as is expedient
to something already given. Rather, they always have already taken us
up into themselves and our thought consists in following their movement. Now, at the end of the two thousand year tradition of Neoplatonism, being captivated by the *logos,* something which the Greeks of
the classical period experienced as *delirium,* and out of which Plato,

in Socrates' name, sees the truth of the Idea emerging, can be seen to be close to the speculative self-movement of the thought as it is explicated in Hegel's dialectic.

Our examination of Hegel's attempt to link himself to the Greeks has thus shown us that there is another place where he and the Greeks converge. It is his affinity with them in the matter of speculation itself, which Hegel half guesses from the Greek texts and half forcibly extracts from them. Here Hegel experiences the linguistic suppleness of Greek thought relative to what is closest to him and most central to his thinking: his own roots in his native tongue, the wisdom of its sayings and its plays on words, and, moreover, in its power of expression in the spirit of Luther, German mysticism, and the Pietist heritage of his Schwabian homeland. To be sure, according to Hegel the form of the statement has no philosophic justification within the body proper of philosophic science. But the cloak of the statement or sentence, just like the word's power of naming, is not simply an empty shell, but a storehouse. It bears and preserves within itself the content for dialectical appropriation and development. Since for Hegel, as we emphasized in the beginning, the adequate formulation of the truth is an unending venture which goes forward only in approximations and repeated attempts, the concretions of the logical instinct in the casing of words, types of statements, and sentences themselves bear the speculative content and indeed are an integral part of the "expression" in which spirit presents itself. Only once we have recognized the proximity of Greek philosophy to Hegel's dialectic in this regard can his reliance upon it be said to rest on a true affinity—one which he himself did not explicitly consider and which is hinted at in his work only now and then in a preliminary way. That affinity exists despite the differences between Hegel and the Greeks created by the methodological ideal of the modern period and despite the violence Hegel does when he claims to see that ideal in the classical tradition. In this regard, one might be reminded of the resemblance between Hegel and his friend, Hölderlin, who, as a poet, assumes a quite similar place in the *querelle des anciens et des modernes*. Hölderlin strove to renew the classical understanding of art in order to give stability and substance to the excessive inwardness of the modern period. For the same reason, the worldly consciousness of the Ancients as it is expressed in the unrestrained daring of their dialectic, stands as a model for thought. But only because the same logical instinct of language is at work in both Hegel and the Greeks, does the paradigm, which Hegel so carefully selects and over which

he attempts to establish the superiority of his own truth of self-con-
scious spirit, retain its true usefulness for his thought. As we saw, it
is not entirely clear to Hegel himself why his "completion" of metaphysics entails a return to its glorious beginnings.

2

Hegel's "Inverted World"

The function of the "inverted world"[1] within the whole of Hegel's history of the experience of consciousness is much more difficult to ascertain than that of almost any other section. Still, for my part, I would characterize this doctrine of the "inverted world" in the chapter on "Force and Understanding" as one of the most central in the structure of the *Phenomenology of Spirit*. I can tie my argument on this point into what R. Wiehl has shown, namely that the beginning of the *Phenomenology* cannot be comprehended at all without direct reference to Kant's philosophy.[2] If one looks at the main divisions of Hegel's phenomenology of consciousness, one cannot help but see that the task he set for himself was to show how the various modes of knowledge, the interaction of which Kant examines—intuition, understanding, and the unity of apperception or self-consciousness—are actually internally related.

In the final analysis, Hegel's chapter on the phenomenology of consciousness is dominated by the question of how consciousness becomes self-consciousness, i.e., how consciousness becomes conscious of the fact that it is self-consciousness. The thesis that consciousness is self-consciousness has been a central doctrine in modern philosophy since Descartes, and thus, Hegel's idea of phenomenology lies in the Cartesian tradition. This is amply demonstrated by parallels in the work of his contemporaries, in particular the largely unknown book by Sinclair, the friend of Hölderlin and Hegel to whom the "Sphragis" in Hölderlin's *Rhein Hymn* is addressed. The book bears the significant title, *Truth and Certainty*. Obviously, with the same intention

1. *Verkehrte Welt.* Any single choice in translating *verkehrt* here is unsatisfactory. For Gadamer's analysis turns on the double sense of the word in German—on the one hand, the value free sense of inverted, backwards, upside down, inside out, etc., and on the other, the evaluative sense of perverted, distorted. In this second sense the thing which is "verkehrt" appears as a caricature of itself. (TRANS.)

2. Cf. R. Wiehl, *Hegel-Studien*, supplement 3, 1964, pp. 103 ff.

as Fichte and at approximately the same time as Hegel, Sinclair attempts to point the way from certainty to truth beginning quite explicitly with the Cartesian concept of *cogito me cogitare*.

Now, when describing the phenomenon of consciousness in his phenomenology of mind or spirit, Hegel assumes from the start that that in which knowing will fulfill itself, that in which alone the concurrence of certainty and truth can be given, cannot merely be consciousness of the objective world which becomes conscious of itself. Rather, it must transcend the ontological status of individual subjectivity. It must be spirit. On the way to this result Hegel's first thesis is: consciousness is self-consciousness. And within Hegel's system the purpose of the first part of the *Phenomenology* is to convincingly justify this thesis. Hegel does this by "demonstrating" the conversion of consciousness into consciousness of itself, i.e., the necessary transition from consciousness to self-consciousness. Thus, Hegel quite consciously makes Kant's conceptual schema—intuition, understanding, and self-consciousness—the basis for his own divisions. It is R. Wiehl's contribution to have shown that in looking back from the chapter on "Force and Understanding," one must view "Sense Certainty" as the point of departure: namely, as consciousness as yet entirely unconscious of its essential self-consciousness.

As a preliminary methodological observation, let me add that we will come to see how Hegel spells out his thesis—and to that end our efforts will be devoted—when we verify in our own experience what Hegel himself requires when he says that everything hinges on the necessity of transitions. We are consciousness looking on. That is the perspective of the *Phenomenology*. And we ourselves must grasp which forms of consciousness appear and in which order they emerge in distinguishing themselves from each other. Hegel's claim that the dialectical transitions are necessary is made good and verified again and again if one reads carefully. Careful reading of him—and not only of him—has the remarkable consequence that precisely that which one extracts in painstaking attempts at interpretation of the section which one is reading, is stated explicitly in the next section. Every reader of Hegel has this experience: the more he explicates the content of a particular train of thought which he has before him, the more certain he can be that that explication will follow in the next section of Hegel's text. That implies that the subject matter of the discussion is always the same and that the same thing is presented on different levels of explication and reveals itself as the proper and single object or content—something of central importance to all philosophy though it is perhaps nowhere as obvious as in Hegel.

At the beginning of the *Phenomenology* this "same thing" takes
the form of consciousness as self-consciousness. Thus, from the start,
one must understand the task which Hegel proposes for himself in the
Phenomenology, namely, to treat self-consciousness, Kant's synthesis
of apperception, not as something previously given, but as something
to be specifically demonstrated as the truth in all consciousness. All
consciousness is self-consciousness. If we recognize this as the theme
then the position in Hegel's system of the chapter on the "inverted
world," which I am about to discuss, becomes clear. It is in the chapter on "Force and Understanding" where the thought-provoking and
startling formulation, "the inverted world" is to be found. Hegel is a
Schwabian and startling people is his passion, just as it is the passion
of all Schwabians. But what he intends here and how he arrives at
this turn of speech is particularly difficult to grasp. I shall attempt to
show how Hegel's "inverted world" might be understood by means of
historical references and in what sense the true world hidden behind
the appearances can be called "inverted."

Our concern here is with the text beginning with Ph 110 ff. The
decisive phrase, "inverted world," follows on page 121. The true
world of which Hegel speaks on page 111 is the world whose inversion,
making it the "inverted world," is set forth on page 121. Here, on page
111, it is not yet recognized as the "inverted world," but rather poses
as the true world and nothing but the truth.

The train of Hegel's thought has led through the determination of
the truth of perception as the concept of force.[3] The perceiving consciousness which the onlooking philosophical consciousness observes
learns that the truth intended by the thesis of the "thing with properties" is not the "thing with properties" but rather force and the play
of forces. As I see it, that is the step which Hegel demands that the
philosophical consciousness grasp. It must realize that the resolution
of the thing into many things—i.e., the atomism resulting when one
approaches what a thing is or its properties are by means of modern
chemical analysis, for example—is not sufficient if one seeks to un-

---

3. Gadamer is referring here to the development in the first chapters of the
Phenomenology, which take consciousness from immediate dependency on
sense data (sense certainty) through more and more mediated forms of knowledge (perception, understanding). The step referred to here is that from knowing a thing with qualities, e.g., salt with the qualities of white, hard, saline taste,
etc., to knowing a universe of objects standing in force relationships to each
other. In Hegel's analysis that is the transition from Perception to Understanding. (TRANS.)

derstand what the reality of the thing and its properties actually is. Perception (*Wahrnehmen*) remains too external. In perceiving, it takes (*nimmt*) properties and things that have properties to be true (*wahr*). But does what is taken in this way to be true, e.g., the chemical structure of things, constitute their entire and true reality? One must see that, in fact, behind these properties there are forces which have their effects in opposition to each other. The formulas of the chemist express the constitution of a substance. But, precisely as the modern development and transformation of chemistry into physics has confirmed, this substance really is a play of forces.

I have now come to the place where a more precise analysis must begin. The dialectic of force is one of those sections of Hegel's work on which he himself has most thoroughly commented, since it not only appears in the *Phenomenology*, but also, in much more lengthy analysis, in the *Logic* and the *Encyclopedia* respectively. It has something so immediately compelling and illuminating about it that Hegel could be said to see what everybody would see if all sophism were dispensed with.

The argument is convincing that a false abstraction is made when one says, "Here is a force which seeks to express itself and which does so when its expression is elicited." To be sure, in this way of putting it the reality of what we have before us would be stated. But, as anyone can see, there is no question that that which elicits an expression of force must in fact be a force itself. What we have before us is thus always a play of forces. In this sense, eliciting and being elicited are the same process. Further, it is equally true—and in this consists the dialectic of force and expression of force—that force is not at all potential force which holds itself back, but rather exists only as its effect. The understanding of this reality as a relationship of self-identical, immutable substances to changing, accidental properties, in fact, proves to be an external one and at that point we become aware of the internal reality of the thing: force. But the assertion that there "exists" a force by itself apart from its expression and isolated from the context of all forces is also a false abstraction. What exists are forces and their interplay. If one examines the forms of consciousness corresponding to these experiences of the object, perception appears to be relating itself to its object externally. It believes it is perceiving the thing which remains the same plus that which changes on its exterior. In comparison to perception, the form of science referred to here as understanding—precisely because it penetrates behind this exterior, strives to get behind it, and searches out the laws governing the forces—has much better comprehension of the real truth.

That is the preparatory step which Hegel takes here (pp. 110 ff). Let me insert ahead of time a general comment about this passage: in analyzing Hegel's *Phenomenology*, one always observes that each new mode of consciousness is presented in two forms. First, in a dialectic or aporetic "for us," Hegel points up the contradiction lying in the presumed object as such and, at the same time, shows how contradictory the consciousness of this object is in the form it presents itself to us. Second, he exhibits the movement in which the consciousness under observation learns of these contradictions itself and is led to abandon its position, i.e., to change its belief about the object; for the object is not at all what it appeared to be. The consequence of this for us observers is that we grasp the necessity of proceeding to a new form of consciousness, and we can expect now that what it believes will actually be the case. It is demonstrated for us that the consciousness, which is given in sense certainty, perception, or understanding, respectively, is not valid. It is not real knowing. Thus we must proceed beyond the consciousness which appears in these forms, for that consciousness involves itself in contradictions which make it impossible for it to stay with the "truth" it had assumed and which make the untruth of its assumptions clear to us. Of course, as whatever particular consciousness it is (e.g., that of the physicist) it persists stubbornly where it finds itself and refuses to move beyond itself. As Hegel puts it, it is forever forgetting what it has learned and thus remains the same form of consciousness. We, the philosophical consciousness, need a better memory and must comprehend that such knowing is not all knowing and the world comprehended by it, not the entire world. Philosophy thus sees the necessity of getting beyond such stubborn consciousness. It is our task here to observe how that transition is accomplished.

What is first developed is the contradiction as it presents itself for us. Properly speaking that is not the dialectic of the phenomenon, for Hegel first treats the contradictions lying in the thought of the object, in its essence. Thus, the dialectic of the essential and inessential, of the thing and its properties, of force and its expression, is a dialectic of the concept and finds its proper place in the *Logic*. The phenomenological insight which Hegel extracts from this subject matter and for the sake of which he develops it, is in respect to knowledge of it: specifically, it is the insight that knowing here must proceed beyond perception if it is to do justice to the task proper to the understanding— finding out what actually is. We are now to look into the inside. At first that is meant quite straightforwardly in comparison to the superficial differentiation of immutable thing and changing properties. If we look in this way into the inside, what do we see? What is the inner essence of the external appearance? One thing is clear: looking into the inside is a matter for the understanding, not sense perception. It is what Plato characterizes as *noein* in contrast to *aisthēsis*. Thus, the object of "pure" thinking (*noein*) is obviously distinguished by the fact that it is not given to the senses.

It is convincing, therefore, when Hegel speaks on page 111 of the "innerly true" as "the *absolute universal,* and thus not merely sense universal, which has developed for the understanding." That is the *noēton eidos,* if I may express myself in Plato's terms for the moment. In it "there now opens up for the first time a supersensible world as the true world above the appearing world." Here is the step which Plato takes.[4] The universal is not the common element in sense appearances which *doxa* has before it. It is the *ontos on,* the *eidos,* the universal of the understanding and not that of the sensuous in its appearing otherness. Hegel's way of building upon this thought has a most singular quality—"above the disappearance of this world, the constant world beyond." Here Plato is made to sound very much like Christianity, and since for Hegel this standpoint is by no means to be the ultimate truth, one can almost hear Nietzsche here and his formulation, "Christianity is Platonism for the masses." Indeed, the structure which Hegel is describing is that of an extreme conceptual abstraction which, as will be demonstrated subsequently, is characteristic not only of the Platonic and Christian position, but also of that of modern science.

The supersensible world is said to be the true world. It is "what remains in disappearnace—a way of putting things often found in Hegel. We will encounter precisely this expression again when we set about understanding the "inverted world." For, to give an indication of where we are headed, it will emerge there that what remains is precisely what is real where everything is continually disappearing. The real world exists precisely as continual change, *constant* change. Constancy, then, is no longer merely the opposite of disappearance, rather, it is the truth of disappearance. That is the thesis of the "inverted world."

How does Hegel reach this conclusion? Here, rather than logically

4. See Hegel's account of Plato's philosophy in his lectures (XIV 169 ff.).

reconstructing his course, I would prefer to bring the phenomenon itself so clearly into focus that we can see just what consciousness supposes as the truth in each truth which consciousness believes it has hold of. R. Wiehl has emphasized correctly that belief always remains present in the form of suppositions or contentions which keep the entire process of exhibiting the forms of consciousness moving. Thus Hegel now raises the question of what it is that consciousness supposes here. What is this inner realm into which the understanding peers? What is this consciousness of the beyond? Is an empty beyond meant? Do we have a prefiguration of the "unhappy consciousness" here?

No, Hegel says, that is not true. This beyond is not empty, for "it comes from appearance"—it is the truth of appearance. What kind of a truth? In answer to that Hegel hits upon a brilliant formulation: the beyond, he says, is the appearance *as* appearance. That is, it is appearance which is not the appearance of something else, and which is no longer to be differentiated from something lying beyond it which is "really." On the contrary, it is nothing but appearance, and thus it is not appearance as opposed to reality, but rather appearance as the real itself. Appearance is a whole of showing (*Schein*), as it is put on page 110. Hegel means here that the appearance is not just an expression of force which, when the force weakens, nullifies itself and its effect. Rather, it is the whole of reality. It not only has its ground; it is as the essence showing itself. As opposed to shallow talk of a thing "having" properties, indeed even as opposed to the insight which penetrates behind that to force which either expresses itself or remains potential, there opens up now a view into the inner essence of things as the "absolute reciprocity" of the play of forces. Here the reality is better comprehended than in the superficial view of perception. Insofar as this play of forces proves to be lawful, the "appearances," *ta phainomena*, are redeemed. "The unity in the play of force itself, and the truth of it, is the law of force" (114). Correspondingly, in the *Logic* it is said of the determinations of reflection that their "showing," i.e., the "showing" of the formal determinations, "consummates itself in appearance" (L II, 101). The phrase, "the whole of showing," leads in this way to the concept of law. One can easily see that the law is something simple in comparison to the shifting interplay of forces affecting each other. As the unitary law, it determines the entirety of appearances. The supposed difference between forces which characterizes their effect—eliciting, being elicited, being potential, being expressed—this difference of the universal, is in fact a unity. This way of putting things is peculiarly Hegelian but the truth of it can be seen and verified in the phenomenon: indeed the difference is in no way one between forces separated from each other, which occur by themselves and which one relates *ex post*. Rather it is the appearance of the simple, identical law.

In what follows, accordingly, the law of nature, the one law fully explaining all phenomena and ultimately dominating the realm of mechanics, emerges as the truth of the object under investigation. That is a most important point. Here one might be reminded of those interpreters of Plato who took Plato's idea for the law of nature. Their view was unintentional Hegelianism, for Hegel himself goes so far as to make this identification. However, it will turn out that he does not stay with it, and we shall see why.[5] In any event, he can say for the time being that the universal difference "is expressed in the law as the constant picture of the fluctuating appearance." The law is what remains in disappearance. Reality is viewed as the world of laws, which remains beyond disappearance. "The supersensible world is thus a tranquil realm of laws"—beyond the perceived world, but present in the latter nevertheless as "its immediate, still image." That is on page 114 f., and here Hegel even speaks of this realm as the still image of constant change.

Unquestionably, this phrase not only sounds like Plato but also like Galileo. Galileo is most certainly there in what follows, or more correctly, Newton. For implied here is obviously the completion of Galileo's system of mechanics with implicit reference to gravity as the universal definition of body. Hegel now demonstrates that the step taken here into the supersensible, true world, the step taken by the understanding, is only a first step which must be recognized as falling short of the whole truth. It is impossible to say that the truth of reality is the natural law. (Natorp, for one, has interpreted Plato as saying this.) Hegel shows, namely, that a formulation such as the "realm of laws" always implies that the whole of appearance is not contained therein. Either consciousness necessarily involves itself in the dialectic of the law and its instances or a multiplication of laws results. *In concreto* one might think here of how Galileo's law of falling bodies was

5. The Marburg school too could not stand pat on this construction of the object through laws. That is demonstrated not only by the later Natorp's concept of *das Urkonkrete* (the originally and ultimately concrete) but also by his understanding of the later Plato, which comes so close to Hegel's. This relationship has been pursued by R. Wiehl in his as yet unpublished studies on Platonic and Hegelian dialectic.

contested by the Aristotelians of his time because it did not explain the whole appearance. Indeed, the whole appearance in this case contains the moment of resistance, of friction. Another law must be added here to the law for free falling bodies, which never exist: the law of friction governing the resistance of the medium. That means that in principle no appearance is a "pure" instance of the law.

In the case of our example we thus have two laws if we actually wish to achieve the goal of portraying the real appearance in the still image of laws. The attempt to extend mechanics in this way in order that it might deal successfully with the "impure" instances of the laws, leads at first to a multiplication of the laws. However, the moving appearances are thereby "understood" essentially as a whole, and thus a vision of the unity in lawfulness opens up, a vision which finds its ultimate realization in the integration of terrestrial physics and celestial mechanics. That, according to Hegel, is what is implied in the thesis of "universal attraction," i.e., the thesis that "everything has a constant difference from everything else." This means that the coincidental determinations based on things as they appear to the senses independently of each other are not the basis for differentiating these things. Rather, the proper basis is the essential determination of every body as constituting a force field. That is the new perspective, from which it is seen that force is essentially not one force in distinction from another, but rather distinguished within itself. Thus electricity, for example, is always positive and negative, i.e., exists as the voltage which we call electric power. To be sure, it exists only in the understanding as this difference in designation. If, for instance, the play of forces is taken as the law of positive and negative electricity, the object intended is the voltage, which is actually electric energy and not two different forces. Thus the truth of the play of forces is the unitary lawfulness of reality, the law of appearance (L II 124 ff.).

There is a dialectic on the side of consciousness corresponding to the dialectic of the object which brought out the untruth in talk of different forces. It is the dialectic of explanation, namely, that the law is different from the reality which it determines only in the understanding. The tautologousness of explanation can be demonstrated using the example of phonetic laws. In this instance one speaks of the laws of modification which "explain" the changes in sound within a language. But the laws, naturally, are nothing other than that which they explain. They do not even hint at making any other claim. All grammatical rules have the same tautological character. In these nothing at all is explained. What in truth is the life of the language, is simply stated as a law governing the language.

I spoke just now of the life of the language intentionally, for our explication is headed in the direction of this concept, and that brings me here to Hegel's doctrine of the "inverted world." For what is always lacking when we allow laws to define changes in appearance? Why do these laws fall short of the true reality? Because change as such is missing in this Platonic-Galilean conception of the tranquil realm of laws or unitary lawfulness. Hegel speaks here of the absoluteness of change, i.e., the principle of alteration. Aristotle had a similar criticism of Plato: the ideas, the *eidē*, he argued, are more *aitia akinēsias ē kinēseōs,* more an answer to the question, "What does *not* change in nature?" than an answer to the question, "What is nature?" For nature as a whole, as Aristotle says, is that which has the *archē tēs kinēseōs en eautō,* that which changes of itself.

Here are Hegel's words at the end of this section, in which the "inverted world" is first mentioned by name (p. 121): "For the first supersensible world was only the *immediate* elevation of the perceived world into the element of the universal"—elevation here to be interpreted as the *ascensus* of Plato's allegory of the "cave," i.e., as an ascent to the noetic world of the permanent idea. "The supersensible world necessarily had its corresponding image in the perceived world." The weakness of the world of ideas is, then, that it is only in opposition to the perceived world taken as unreal. Aristotle's objection to Plato's doubling of the world is meant similarly. Why this copy of the perceived world? Why the noetic world? Is not the mathematically figured world lacking in what is most important? Is it not the "true world" only *for* this changing, moving, perceived world, and does it not lack the principle of change and alteration which constitutes the being of the perceived world after all?[6] Accordingly, Hegel concludes, "The first realm of laws was lacking in this, but as the inverted world it now contains it." A world which contains the *archē kinēseōs,* and as such is the true world, is an inversion of Plato's world in which motion and alteration were supposed to be naught. This world too is

6. This would seem to be the place to point to the ambivalence in Hegel's understanding of Plato. On the one hand, he views him with the eyes of Aristotle: "Plato expresses the essence rather more as the universal and thus the element of reality seems to be missing in him." On the other hand, he recognizes in Plato's dialectic this "negative principle" (i.e., of reality) when he says that principle essentially touches upon reality "if it is the unity of what is opposed" (XIV 322).

supersensible, that is, the alterations here are not merely "different" and hence unreal, but rather are understood *as motions*. This world is not just the tranquil realm of laws which all alteration must obey, rather it is a world in which everything moves because everything contains the origin of change in itself. That appears to be a pure reversal, and modern philosophical research has also struck upon the image of "reversal" for Aristotle's reinterpretation of Plato's doctrine of ideas. The *tode ti*, not the highest *eidos*, is the primary substance (J. Stenzel).

But to what extent does this reversal in ontological emphasis justify calling the true world *verkehrt* in the sense of "perverted"? What form does this second supersensible world take? To achieve complete clarity here I must return to what was under consideration before. As an example of differential in force Hegel uses electricity, which he formalizes as the dialectic of what is of the same and different names. That dialectic appears in electricity as the difference between positive and negative. Hegel's example, however, need not limit us. What Hegel illustrates at any given point with a particular example is often also substantiated in other "spheres." Here the expression "of the same name" shall be our guide. In Greek what is of the same name (homonymous) is called *homōnumon* or in Latin, *univocum*. That of the same name is, if viewed scholastically, the genus. Law and genus are here to be taken as one—they both are characterized by the fact that properly speaking they *exist* only as their various instances. To be clear about this one should say that that of the same name stands in need of, that is, refers to that named differently. The genus of hoofed animals refers to horses, donkeys, mules, camels, etc. The differently named species are what the genus means, its truth. And similarly, each single species refers to the different individuals. If we think that through, we are led to the ultimate conclusion that the difference or what is different, i.e., that which is neither expressed nor contained in that of the same name, is precisely what is real. Again we recognize a theme from antiquity, for this point is basic to Aristotle's criticism of Plato's "idea" and to Aristotle's own teaching. The *eidos* is only an aspect of the *tode ti:* or, as Hegel will put it (p. 124), this "inverted" supersensible world contains the world which it inverts. It contains the *eidos* as *what* constitutes the "this-here" in the *tode ti* and which alone provides the answer to the question which the understanding raises, namely, *ti esti?* (cf. Aristotle's *Categories*). Aristotle too cannot answer this differently from Plato. When I have a this-something before me and am asked, "What is it?" I can only answer with the *eidos*. In this sense the standpoint of the understanding is all-inclusive. But that does not mean that reality is only the *eidos*. Quite the opposite: what is real is the individual which is "of this species" and of which it can be said that it is of this type. But how can Hegel assert that this appearing existent contains its reversal in itself as a perversion? Why is the true reality called the *verkehrte* world?

I would like to pursue a line of thought here which will make the concept of the inverted or perverted world, respectively, comprehensible. What appears in one way or another is never "pure" *eidos*, although the *eidos* is only present in appearance. As Leibniz puts it, no egg is like another. No instance is a pure case of a law. The real world as it exists in opposition to the "truth" of the law is thus perverted. Things do not occur in it in a way that would correspond to the ideas of an abstract mathematician or a moralist. Indeed, the live reality of it consists precisely in its perversion. And that is its function in the *Phenomenology*'s dialectical process of demonstration—the end result will be that being inverted in itself is being turned towards itself or relating itself to itself, and that, precisely, is the structure of Life.

But does Hegel really have a sense of being inverted as being wrong in mind? Does he not always mean the dialectical reversal and does he not want to say here too that the true world is not that supersensible world of tranquil laws, but rather the reverse of this? That of the similar which is dissimilar, the changing, is the truth—in this sense inversion constitutes the essence of one side of the supersensible world (p. 123). But Hegel cautions quite expressly that the matter cannot be imagined in a physical sense, as though it were a case of the inversion (reversal) of something established, i.e., as though there were a supersensible world to begin with and then also a second inverted one. As stated on page 123, the reversal is much more reflection into self and not opposition of one thing to another. The dialectical point of this reversal is obviously that when I take the opposite (the inverted-perverted world) to be true "in and for itself," the truth is necessarily the opposite of itself. For in what it is in and for itself the reality of appearance had, in fact, proven to be more than the pure instances of laws. That implies, however, that that reality is also the law of appearance. It is both: the law and the perversion of the law. It is the opposite of itself. If we take as our example for this Hegel's critique of thought-things which only ought to be, of the hypotheses and all the other "invisible truths of an ever recurring ought" (Ph 190), then, indeed, the reasonable view of reality would reject the vacuous universality of such hypotheses and laws even though reality includes these. What is reasonable and concrete is the reality determined by the principle of change. Abstractions are always confounded because things never turn out as one thought they would.

As is common knowledge, the *Logic* contains the complete development of thought's determinations of being. For this reason it is the natural commentary on the opinions about objective being found in the forms of consciousness developed in the *Phenomenology*. The "inverted world" is also to be found not only in the *Phenomenology* but in the *Logic* too and, specifically, in a form there such that the world in and for itself is the inversion of the world which appears. Obviously reversal is the basic meaning here and nothing here could mislead one into thinking that a perversion of this world in any substantive sense is meant. Still it must not be forgotten that the *Encyclopedia* (also the Heidelberg version) never makes use of the concept of the "inverted world" at all and that the *Logic* develops the dialectic of this concept in a way not entirely consistent with the *Phenomenology*.

It seems as if Hegel might have recognized that the abstract juxtaposition of law and appearance as it is presented in the *Phenomenology*, i.e., as the opposition of the supersensible and sense world, is not at all in keeping with the meaning of law. In the *Phenomenology* he says of the tranquil realm of laws that, though to be sure it is beyond the perceived world, it is also present in the latter as its immediate, still image. However, he says in the same context in the *Logic*, "The law is *not* beyond the appearance, but rather present in it immediately" (L II 127).[7] Corresponding to this, the realm of laws no longer appears in the *Logic* as a *world*, supersensible or otherwise. "The existing world is itself the realm of the laws."

Of course the concept of law goes through the same stages here as in the *Phenomenology*. It is at first the mere basis of appearance and constitutes what stays the same in change—alongside of which the changing content of appearance continues to exist. We have a second step and a changed sense of law when the law itself presupposes the differences which constitute its content. In substance these stages correspond to the first and second supersensible worlds of the *Phenomenology*. But, significantly, only at this point is it said that the law in which the totality of appearance in itself is reflected, has the character of totality, i.e., is a world. In the *Logic*, namely, the tranquil realm of laws is not called the supersensible *world*: "world" first appears in the "world" which is inverted, i.e., totally reflected

7. My italics.

into itself and existing in and for itself, or what is called in the *Phenomenology* the *second supersensible world*. [8] Only of the latter is it said expressly, "Thus the appearance reflected into itself is now a world, which opens up as existing in and for itself above the appearing world." It is also called the supersensible world (L II 131 f.), and finally proves to be the "inverted world." Many of Hegel's examples of its inversion used here and in the *Phenomenology*, that is, examples for the reversal of the supersensible world, are of no help to us in clarifying the general sense of *verkehrt*. North pole and south pole, positive and negative electricity, illustrate only that these relationships can be turned around and accordingly have a dialectical character (Ph 122; L II 134).

Still the question persists whether the phrase *verkehrte Welt* as much as it might have the dialectical meaning of "turned around" might nevertheless not also connote for Hegel something in line with a double sense of both inverted and perverted. I find a first indication that it does on page 122 of the *Phenomenology*. There one comes across the phrase, ". . . the law of a world which has opposite it a *verkehrte* supersensible world in which that which is scorned in the first is honored in the second and vice versa." The *verkehrte* world is thus a world in which everything is the reverse of the right world. Isn't that a familiar principle of literature, one which we call satire? One might be reminded in this regard of Plato's myths, in particular, of that in the *Statesman,* and of that master of English satire, Swift. Further, as is hinted in the figure of speech, "that's a topsy-turvy world" (*verkehrte Welt*), meaning, for example, when servants play masters and masters, servants, this kind of reversal is illuminating in some way. What is found in the topsy-turvy world is not simply the contrary, the mere abstract opposite of the existent world. Rather this reversal in which everything is the opposite of itself makes visible in a kind of fun house mirror the covert perversion of everything as we know it. If this is so, the topsy-turvy world would be the perversion of perversity. Being the perverted world backwards would amount to displaying the perversion of the latter *e contrario*. And that is certainly the point of all satire.

Such portrayal in a counterfactual possibility illumines for a moment a valid though unreal possibility in the established world as it stands, Indeed, this is precisely the purpose of satirical portrayal. As a form of statement, satirical inversion presupposes that the world

8. My italics.

will recognize in the reversal of itself its own perversion and thus come to see its true possibilities. Thus, it is the real world itself which splits apart into possibility and counter-possibility. In that the topsy-turvy world displays itself as reversed, it exhibits the wrongness of the established world as it stands. Thus Hegel can justifiably say that this world is "perverted (*verkehrt*) for itself, i.e., the perversion of itself," for it is no mere opposite. The true world, on the contrary, is both the truth projected as an ideal and its own perversion. Now if we keep in mind too that one of the main tasks of satire is to expose moral hypocrisy, i.e., the untruth of the world as it is supposed to be, the real trenchancy of *verkehrt* comes into view. The perversion of the true reality becomes visible behind its false front since in every instance satirical portrayal is the "opposite in itself," whether this takes the form of exaggeration, innocence in contrast to hypocrisy, or whatever.[9]

It is in this sense that the *verkehrte* world is more than a direct opposite of what appears. Hegel states specifically (p. 122) that any view would be superficial in which "the one world is the appearance; the other, the in-itself." That is an opposition which the understanding supposes, but, in truth, it is not a matter here of the opposition of two worlds. Rather, it is the "true, supersensible" world which contains both aspects and which divides itself into this opposition and thereby relates itself to itself.

This interpretation is particularly well documented by a recurring theme in Hegel, one of his favorites, which concerned him from his youth on. It is the problem of punishment and the forgiveness of sins, respectively—a problem which forced the young theologian, Hegel, beyond Kant's and Fichte's moral conception of the world. And, as a matter of fact, to my knowledge the idea of inversion-

---

9. The literary use of the concept of the "inverted world" in the satire of the late middle ages is set forth in *extenso* by Karl Rosenkranz in his *Geschichte der deutschen Poesie im Mittelalter,* Halle, 1830, pp. 586–94. See also Klaus Lazarowicz, *Vekehrte Welt. Vorstudien zu einer Geschichte der deutschen Satire,* Tübingen, 1963, which to be sure does not trace the history of this turn of speech. Somewhat more is to be found in Alfred Liede, *Dichtung als Spiel. Unsinnspoesie an den Grenzen der Sprache,* Berlin, 1963, vol. 2, pp. 40 ff., and some evidence for my thesis from the seventeenth century, in Jean Rousset, *La littérature de l'âge baroque,* Paris, 1963, pp. 26–28, in particular, p. 27, according to which it would appear that the folk motif of a turnabout into the absurd only gradually assumes the character of a statement of the truth in the sense of satire.

perversion is first found in Hegel's analysis of the problem of punishment.[10] As the *Phenomenology* expressly states, it would be simplistic
if one were to take punishment to be punishment only in appearance
here, and, in reality or in another world, to be for the benefit of the
criminal (p. 122). Only the abstract thinking of the understanding
permits such talk of two worlds and in this account of things there is
no speculative reversal. The reversal which punishment implies is also
not that of an actual countereffect against which the wrongdoer seeks
to defend himself. That would not be the position of justice at all but
rather one of vindictiveness. Of course there is such an immediate law
of retribution. But punishment has a meaning quite the opposite of
this and thus in Hegel it is called the "inversion" of revenge. The individual seeking revenge holds himself to be the essential concern in
opposition to the violator and seeks to restore his injured existence
through destruction of the wrongdoer. But the concern in punishment
is a quite different one, namely, with a violation of law. The countereffect of the penalty is not a mere consequence of the violation, rather it belongs to the very essence of the misdeed. The misdeed as a
crime demands punishment, which is to say that it does not have the
immediacy of a simple action, but rather exists in the form of universality as crime *per se*. Thus Hegel is able to say that, ". . . the inversion of it (*Verkehrtheit derselben*) is the punishment, i.e., that the
crime becomes the opposite of what it was previously." Punishment
as inversion (*Verkehrtheit*) plainly implies that punishment has an
essential tie to the misdeed. Punishment is reasonable. The wrongdoer, as the reasonable man he wants to be, must turn against himself. In the *System of Ethicality* Hegel describes most impressively
how this reversal comes to pass abstractly and ideally in the phenomenon of the bad conscience.[11] The wrongdoer's sensitivity to the division within himself may be anesthetized again and again by the fear
of punishment and also by his resistance to its impending reality, but
it always returns in the ideal realm of conscience. That means that the
wrongness of the deed shows up again and again as long as the punishment is "called for."

But then is it not necessary to take the turning around as it occurs
here in relationship to punishment in the double sense which the full

10. Hegel, *Theologische Jugendschriften,* ed. H. Nohl, Tübingen, 1907, p. 280.
11. Hegel, *Schriften zur Politik und Rechtsphilosophie,* ed. George Lasson,
Leipzig, 1913, p. 453.

meaning of *Verkehrtheit* would imply? That the punishment is required as the necessary inversion of the misdeed means that it is
recognized as that inversion. In it, therefore, the reconciliation of the
law with the reality of crime opposed to it has occurred. If it is accepted and carried out and thus becomes actual punishment, it cancels itself out and correspondingly the self-destruction of the criminal
ends and he is again one with himself. With his acceptance of his fate,
the dichotomy prevailing in his existence—on the one hand the fear
of punishment, on the other, the pangs of conscience—is eliminated.
Here, too, one can say that the *verkehrte* world in which punishment
"is not that which damages and annihilates a man, but rather an extension of grace which preserves man's essence," is not simply an inversion of the abstract world where misdeed and punishment are
opposed. It also reveals the perversity of that abstract world and elevates it to the "higher sphere"[12] of fate and reconciliation with fate.

The further sequence of the forms of knowledge in the *Phenomenology* also makes it quite clear that "*Verkehrung*" and "*Verkehrtheit*" refer specifically and above all to what is good and evil, and,
thus, that the meaning of "*Verkehrt*" is as much substantive as it is
formal. In the chapter "Culture and the Realm of Reality" the example used in the *Logic* for the "*Verkehrte Welt*" is made thematic,
specifically the fact that "what in phenomenal existence is evil, misfortune, etc., is in and for itself good and fortunate" (L II 134).
There it is said that,

> When the upright consciousness, in the only way possible for
> it here, makes itself the guardian of the good and noble, (i.e.,
> of that which remains constant throughout all expression of
> itself), in order that the good and noble not be *linked* to the
> bad or *mixed* with it. ... this consciousness, though it thinks
> it is refuting the fact, has only restated in a trivial way, ...
> that the noble and good is essentially the inversion-perversion
> of itself, just as the bad is conversely the most admirable. (Ph
> 373 f.)

The good *is* the bad. One cannot take Hegel literally enough here.
"*Summum ius—summa inuria*" means that abstract justice is perversion of justice, that it not only leads to injustice but is itself ultimate
injustice. We are far too accustomed to reading speculative statements

---

12. Hegel, *Theologische Jugendschriften*, p. 279.

as if there were a subject underlying them to which only different characteristics are attributed.[13]

At this point we return from our investigation of the dialectical sense of the "inverted-perverted world" to our consideration of its function in the *Phenomenology*'s train of thought. For my demonstration I have used the example of punishment and acceptance of fate, which came, to be sure, from "another sphere"—one, however, which Hegel himself brings in as an illustration (Ph 122). But though the example is from "another sphere," the structure and inner necessity of the dialectical development which concerns us is confirmed by it. We have no choice but to admit that the unsensed, supersensible world of the universal represents only an aspect of that which really is. The true reality is that of life, which moves itself within itself. Plato conceived of this as the *autokinoun*, Aristotle, as the essence of *physis*. In the progression of the forms of knowing which the *Phenomenology* traverses, an enormous step is made here, where the being of what lives is grasped. What lives is not an instance of law or the composite result of laws bearing on each other, rather it is turned towards itself or it relates itself: it behaves. It is a self. There is an enduring truth here. For however far modern physiology might go in unlocking the secret of organic life, in knowing what lives we will never cease to make a turnabout in our thinking of that which, as the play of forces, lawfully determines organic nature: we will think of it, conversely, as the behavior of the organism and "understand" this organism as living. Though a Newton of the blade of grass may one day appear, in a deeper sense Kant will prove to be right. Our understanding of the world will not cease to judge "teleologically." For us, and not only for Hegel, the transition here is necessary, i.e., the progression to another, higher form of knowing as well as to a higher form of what is known. Indeed, in a decisive sense, that which we look upon as living we must view as a self. A "self," however,

---

13. See chapter 1 above. In passing it should be mentioned that ordinary German usage quite confidently distinguishes between *falsch* (false) and *verkehrt* (inverted or backwards). Of course an answer which inverts things or gets them twisted is not correct, but the elements of truth are recognizable in it and only need to be put right. A false answer, on the other hand, contains no such possibility of making it right. Thus, for example, the information someone gives you can be called *falsch* if it is deliberately given with the intent of deceiving—but in such a case it could not be called *verkehrt*. For an answer which is *verkehrt* is always one which was meant to be correct and which turned out to be false. In this sense too the *malum* is the *conversio boni*.

means self-identity in all undifferentiatedness and all self-differentiation. The mode of being of what lives corresponds in this to the mode
of being of the knowledge which understands what lives. For consciousness of what is as a self has the same structure of differentiation
which is no differentiation. Thus the transition to self-consciousness
has been essentially completed. We must now grasp that the "inverted
world" is in fact the real world—even if in the eyes of the idealist and
mathematical physicist it is impure and therefore perverted since the
abstract universality of the law and its pure instances are not present
in it. That means that there is life in it which maintains itself in infinite change, in the continuing differentiation of itself from itself. And
once we have acknowledged this, the mediation which Hegel undertakes in his dialectical exposition of consciousness has been essentially
achieved. It has been demonstrated, then, that consciousness is self-
consciousness. In its knowing consciousness is actually more sure of
this than of all conceptions of what is which have been mediated by
the senses and the understanding. This certainty goes byond all of
these conceptions. For if it thinks of what is, as a self, that is, as that
which relates itself to itself, what it thinks of is intended as something
which has the same certainty of itself which consciousness has. That
is the true penetration into the interior of nature, which alone is able
to grasp the "natural" in nature, i.e., its life. The living feels the living—it understands it from the inside as it understands itself as a self.
The *autokinoun*, abstractly defined, is the act of the living self relating
itself to itself. Expressed as knowing, it is the formula of idealism, I =
I, self-consciousness.

Thus, the first part of the *Phenomenology* has achieved the goal of
pointing out to consciousness that it contains the standpoint of idealism within itself. What leads Hegel beyond the standpoint of idealism,
specifically the concept of reason which transcends the subjectivity of
the self and which is realized as spirit, has been given a foundation in
this first section. Realization of that concept even now exceeds our
grasp.

3

Hegel's Dialectic of Self-consciousness

The following essay treats one of the most famous chapters in Hegel's philosophy.[1] Paradoxically, the passionate dedication to freedom which characterized the era of revolutions in Europe and which was Hegel's passion too, seems to be responsible for the fact that this chapter's true value in showing the nature and reality of freedom has not been comprehended. It is necessary, therefore, that in attempting to critically clarify its meaning, we guard against the effect of the excessively resounding slogan, "freedom." To this end it is wise to carefully consider the importance of this chapter's position in the chain of demonstration in Hegel's science of appearing spirit. I shall begin, accordingly, by showing that Hegel knows full well what he is after when he refuses to introduce transcendental idealism in the manner of Fichte, who, for his part, claims to think Kant to his conclusion.

What does it mean when Hegel asserts, "that not merely is consciousness of a thing only possible for self-consciousness, but that the latter alone is the truth of such forms" (Ph 128)? A different problem is posed here from the one Kant poses and solves in his transcendental deduction of the pure concepts of the understanding. To be sure, the transcendental synthesis of apperception is a function of self-consciousness, but only insofar as it always makes the consciousness of something else, an object, possible. And even that consciousness of the self-determination of reason which Fichte's "Doctrine of Science" develops out of the primacy of practical reason has a transcendental function and serves as a basis for knowledge of the "not-I." Opposed to this stands Hegel's emphatic declaration that in self-consciousness the concept of spirit has been reached and, thus, the turning point where consciousness "steps out of the varicolored appearance of the sensuous 'here'

---

1. Hegel, *Phenomenology of Mind,* chapter 4: "Self-consciousness": "The Truth and Certainty of Itself," and "The Independence and Dependence of Self-consciousness: Mastery and Servitude" (Ph 133–50).

and the empty night of the supersensible 'beyond' into the spiritual daylight of the present" (Ph 140). In the overtones of Hegel's baroque formulation one detects that in the concept of spirit a reality has been reached which, like the light of day, embraces everything visible and includes all there is. That gives the chapter on "self-consciousness" a central position within the whole of the path traversed in the *Phenomenology*. To be sure, self-consciousness is an immediate certainty, but that this certainty of self-consciousness is at the same time the truth of all certainty is at this point not yet contained in its immediate certainty as such. Hegel expressly points to the fact that even that idealism which calls itself transcendental philosophy and which asserts its certainty of being all reality, in fact recognizes another certainty: in Kant, the "thing in itself," in Fichte, the "impetus" (*Anstoss*). Thus Hegel can say that "the idealism which begins with this assertion is a form of pure assurance, which neither comprehends itself nor can make itself comprehensible to others" (177). I wish to shed some light upon the difference it makes when, following Hegel, one conceives of the way of true idealism as the way from consciousness to self-consciousness. How is the certainty of consciousness that it is all reality thereby demonstrated? And does this certainty surpass not only Kant's transcendental deduction, but also Fichte's absolute idealism of freedom?

One should keep in mind that Schelling too thought that the standpoint of idealism lacked a substantial proof and considered the "I" of intellectual intuition and of self-consciousness to be the higher potency, the potentiated subject-object of nature. Of course Hegel, here in his *Phenomenology of Spirit,* criticizes Schelling's concept of the absolute because of what the former considered the lack of mediation in its absoluteness. But the way in which Hegel derives the idealism of reason here and opposes it to transcendental or formal idealism, reaffirms Schelling's concern and not merely in the way Hegel had done when he had previously attempted to mediate and surpass Fichte's and Schelling's systems in his essay on their "difference."[2] As a matter of fact, in Hegel's subsequent system of philosophic sciences as well, he develops nature as the real foundation of spirit's actualization of itself. And in the later systematic ordering, the "phenomenology" is a part of this philosophy of reality insofar as it is the science of appearing and therefore real spirit. Thus the

2. Hegel, *Differenz des Fichte'schen und Schelling'schen Systems der Philosophie,* Hamburg, 1962.

merely formal principle of idealism has no place at all in the science
of real spirit or, more to the point, that formal principle is made
actual in that science insofar as self-consciousness is not merely the
individual point of consciousness's certainty of itself, but rather
reason. That means that thought is certain that it is experiencing the
whole world "as its own truth and presence." In this way Hegel trans-
forms Kant's problem of the transcendental deduction of the concepts
of the understanding and "proves" the idealism of reason via the certainty of self-consciousness.

For reason is not only in thought. Hegel defines reason as the unity
of thought and reality. Thus, implied in the concept of reason is that
reality is not the other of thought and, hence, that the opposition of
appearance and understanding is not a valid one. Reason is certain of
all that: "To it (self-consciousness), in that it so conceives of itself, it
seems as if the world only now had come into being for it. Before
this, it does not understand the world. It desires and works on it,
withdraws from it and draws back into itself . . ." (176). Thus Hegel
is describing the path on which "empty" idealism elevates itself to the
idealism of reason. That everything is "mine" as the content of my
consciousness is not yet the truth of this consciousness. As Hegel expresses it, "Self-consciousness has only come into existence for itself,
and does not yet exist as unity with consciousness in general" (128).
We can also say that in the individual point of its self-certain self, its
true essence as spirit and reason is not yet recognized.

It is determined in subsequent stages of appearing spirit that self-
consciousness does not yet exist in its truth as long as it is the mere
individual point of certainty of itself, i.e., that it is the whole of reality only in unity with consciousness. But first a more precise analysis
is required of the transition into this sphere. In our examination of
the "inverted-perverted world"[3] we said that the world of the laws
of force was "perverted" precisely because "the perceptual image
establishing the differences in another element of existence" remains
to be removed there. The point is that the *chorismos* and the
Platonic hypostasizing of ideas needs to be dispensed with just as
does the claim that nature can be explained by "principia mathe-
matica." Ontologically, the difference between idea and appearance
is as invalid as that between the understanding and what it explains.
It is a serious mistake to see this doctrine of the "inverted-
perverted world" as a critique, or worse, a caricature of the

3. See above, chapter 2.

sciences, for it is not at all inappropriate to assert that when it is "explaining," consciousness is in "immediate discussion with itself" (127). In contrast, the truth of positivism is precisely that it replaces the concept of explanation with that of description—as Kirchhoff's famous formulation expresses it.[4] In essence, Hegel has grasped this correctly. The dichotomization of reality into universal and particular, idea and appearance, the law and its instances, needs just as much to be eliminated as does the division of consciousness into consciousness on the one side and its object on the other. What is then thought of in the new way is termed the "inner difference" or "infinitude" by Hegel. Specifically, insofar as that which differentiates itself within itself is not limited from the outside by the boundary of something else from which it differentiates itself, it is infinite in itself. And I have shown that it is the concept of a self which possesses this infinitude, a concept just as much essential to life, the being of organic things which behave and enter into relationships, as it is to the consciousness of itself had by the I which understands itself, i.e., this form of "repulsion of what has the same name, taken as what has the same name, from itself."

It has become clear "for us" that this other is not another: "I who am of the same name, repel myself from myself" (128). But the repulsion of what has the same name and the attraction of what is named differently is not only the structure of self-consciousness, but also of the physical tension of electromagnetic phenomena and of the Platonic differentiation of idea from the appearance which participates in the idea as that of the same name. Hegel uses the concept of the homonymous abstractly here, so that it embraces both Plato's doctrine of ideas (*homōnumon*) as well as the modern concept of law and the electromagnetic equation. The self-referentiality characterizing self-consciousness is thus a truth for the understanding, but as an event in which it does not recognize itself. As soon as consciousness acquires a concept of this infinitude, it is no longer understanding, but rather appears in the form of self-consciousness. That point is reached at the level of life and knowledge of it. He who grasps the behavior of what is alive, i.e., grasps it as differentiation of the undifferentiated, must first already know himself, i.e., be self-consciousness; but beyond this, he will ultimately come to the insight that his own forms of consciousness, whose truth had been a thing other than these

4. Cf. G. R. Kirchhoff, *Vorlesungen über mathematische Physik und Mechanik,* Leipzig, 1874, preface.

forms themselves, are not different at all from their other (which is consciousness too) but undifferentiatedly one with it. Thus these forms are self-consciousness. The truth does not, as the understanding presumed, lie "beyond" in the supersensible, in the "inner," rather consciousness is itself this "inner," which is to say it is self-consciousness.

It is clear then that what appears as this differentiation of the undifferentiated has life's structure of splitting in two and becoming identical with itself. That, Hegel worked out in those pages preserved through fortunate coincidence from his Frankfurt years. Life is the identity of identity and difference. Everything alive is bound to its "other," the world around it, in the constant exchange of assimilation and secretion. And beyond this, the individual living thing does not exist as an individual, but rather only as the mode in which the species preserves itself. Thus it bespeaks neither a lack of clarity nor arbitrariness on Hegel's part when, in the *Phenomenology,* the universal structure of life as inner difference or infinity is developed both at the end of the chapter on consciousness and the beginning of the chapter on self-consciousness: on the one hand, as the final development in the way the understanding thinks and, on the other, under the title, "Determination of Life," as an adumbration of the structure of self-consciousness. That is not a mere anthropomorphism which modern behavioral research would point out as such to man's humiliation. Rather, there is a methodologically compelling state of affairs here. Self-consciousness governs necessarily whenever any attempt at all is made to think what behavior is. Furthermore, in proceeding from the other side of this parallelism, we see that the structural identity between the life processes of what lives and self-consciousness demonstrates that self-consciousness is not at all the individualized point of "I = I," but rather, as Hegel says, "the I which is we and the we which is I" (Ph 140), which is to say, spirit. To be sure, Hegel first makes that assertion in the introduction to the dialectic of self-consciousness. For it is only clear "for us," for reflecting or observing consciousness, that life, the unity of the different, will also prove to be the truth of self-consciousness, namely, that it is all reality and hence reason. Hegel is seeking a kind of reconciliation here between the "anciens" and the "modernes." For Hegel there is no opposition between existing reason, existing spirit, *logos, nous,* and *pneuma,* on the one hand, and the *cogito,* the truth of self-consciousness, on the other. The course of appearing spirit is the course which Hegel follows in teaching us to recognize the standpoint of the "anciens" in the standpoint of the "modernes."[5]

When Hegel says that in reaching self-consciousness we have now entered the homeland of truth, he means that truth is no longer like the foreign country of otherness into which consciousness seeks to penetrate. It had only seemed so from the standpoint of consciousness. Now, in contrast, consciousness as self-consciousness is a native of the land of truth and is at home in it. For one thing, it finds all truth in itself. For another, however, it knows that it embraces the entire profusion of life within itself.

At this point there is no longer need for an exact analysis of the sides of the dialectic constituting the cycle of life—the dialectic between the single exemplar and the species, the single creature and the whole. To know its result is sufficient for us, namely, the "reflected unity." What, on the one hand, is the "immediate continuity and homogeneity of its being" ("universal blood"), and on the other, has "the form of that which exists for itself discretely," and is also the pure process of both of these—in short, the "entirety which maintains itself simply in this movement"—is determined as the unitary species itself (138). What is alive is the species and not the individual. In other words, as life, it is a reflected unity for which the differences of the exemplars are no differences.

It is easy to see that the "I" has the same structure as this. For the "I" as well, the differences are no differences—all that exists are the "I's" representations. But more than this structural identity is manifest here. That which is a self-consciousness is itself necessarily life. Thus Hegel speaks specifically of this "other life." But, as self-consciousness, this "other life" is a special kind of life, namely, one which has consciousness and for which, accordingly, the species character of all that lives is "given." It itself is not only a species in structure, that is, as "I," it is not only in fact the simple universal unifying in itself everything different; rather, it knows "for itself" that all other life is just species, while as self-consciousness it alone is "species for itself." The first immediate evidence of this is that it knows nothing other than itself. The "nullity of the other" fills it completely—quite like it fills life, incidentally, which knows nothing other than itself and maintains itself as individual by dissolving everything else, i.e., inorganic substance, in itself and which maintains itself as species in

5. See above, chapter 1.

careless profligacy and sacrifice of the individual. As self-consciousness it is conscious of this nullity of the other and proves this nullity
to itself by destroying the other. That is its first mediation, through
which self-consciousness "produces" itself as "true" certainty, as
desire—a self-consciousness which Hegel refers to on occasion as the
"unadulterated feeling of self" (148). For in fact, in its immediacy it
is the vital certainty of being alive; in other words, it has the confirmation of itself which it gains through the satisfaction of desire.

But at this point a "however" is required which qualifies the truth
of this self-consciousness. It is all too clear that the self-consciousness
of desire or of satisfaction of desire, respectively, provides no lasting
certainty, for "in pleasure I thirst for desire."[6] Faust's unhappy odyssey through the world provides him with no fulfillment at all. That in
which desire finds its satisfaction is, as long as desire is nothing other
than desire, necessarily something to be destroyed and rendered
nothing, and thus it is nothing at all. For that reason the self-consciousness which desires does not find anything in this way in which
it could feel confirmed. On the contrary, it needs to experience that
the object can stand on its own (135). For us that is quite evident.
We, who have followed the course of the *Phenomenology of Spirit* to
this point, know, of course, that the self-consciousness of being alive
is not a true, substantial self-consciousness. All it "knows" is that as
something alive its identity consists only in constant annulment of
the other and dissolution of self in the other, i.e., in participation in
the infinity of the cycle of life.

Consequently, the object of desire is itself "life"—precisely because the object for the consciousness of desire is "everything else"
besides that consciousness, the latter being the self. That is pointed
out in Hegel's dialectic when he raises the question of how the self-
consciousness of desire comes to learn of the independence of its object. Hegel's meaning is not only that this other which desire annihilates exists independently of it in the sense that the object of desire
is always brought into existence again whenever desire reignites. Beyond this, he is asserting that the object of desire as such, i.e., as it
is, not only for us, but for desire itself, has the structure of life. The
exact sense of this must be understood. Plainly, the point is that it is
not this or that specific thing, but rather something relatively indifferent, which on any given occasion, in being the object of desire and
by providing satisfaction for the latter, gives one certainty of oneself.

6. Goethe, *Faust,* 3250.

Desire is as little interested in the differences which various "objects" might have as the species is in the life of the individual, or the organism in the particular foodstuffs which it assimilates. He who is hungry wants "something to eat"—it does not matter what. Still, the self-consciousness of desire remains tied to this other: "for there to be this cancellation, this other must exist" (139). To this extent, the object stands on its own: "it is indeed something different from self-consciousness, the essence desire." One must take this statement at full value. It means that the feeling of self in desire, the latter igniting and going out as it does, is not at all the truth of self-consciousness which it appeared to be. On the contrary, the self-consciousness of desire knows itself to be dependent on the object of desire as something other than itself. "The certainty of self reached in its satisfaction" is conditioned by the object. It is indeed an "other" which desire wants. Only if this other exists can self-consciousness find satisfaction in negating it. Of course the particular object of desire being annihilated no longer has self-sufficiency, for that is precisely what it loses. That which satiates our hunger and thirst is a mere other, of which we are the negation. But for just that reason this sensuous feeling of self is not true self-consciousness. The condition of animal desire, for example, that of extreme hunger or thirst, consists, to be sure, in knowing nothing other than oneself. But it is not a coincidence that we speak in this regard of being as hungry as a bear or wolf—hunger predominates here to the extent that nothing fills us other than what fills an animal absorbed in the single dimension of its instinctual drives. And for that reason the animal does not, properly speaking, possess a consciousness of itself. That is evidenced by the fact that the satisfaction of desire cancels itself as self-consciousness. In order that desire might attain true self-consciousness, the object of desire must, in all of its "nothingness of the other," still not cease to exist. It must be living self-consciousness in the "particularity of its distinctness" (140). To be sure, as desire, the desire seeking real self-consciousness also knows only itself and seeks nothing but itself in the other. But such desire is only able to find itself in the other if this other is independent and grants that it does not exist in its own right, but rather that, in disregard of itself, it "is for another" (139). Only consciousness is able to be the other of itself in this way and to cancel itself in such a fashion that it does not cease to exist. It is in this sense that self-consciousness "must" get its satisfaction and the object "must" of itself carry out the negation of itself. The "must" here is the classical *ex hypotheseōs anagkaion* found in Aristotle: if self-consciousness is to become true self-consciousness, then it must stand on its own and find another self-consciousness that is willing to be "for it." Thus, the doubling of self-consciousness is a necessary consequence: self-consciousness is only possible as double. It also learns that fact from its experience. Only something which in spite of being negated is still there, in other words, only what negates itself, can by its existence confirm for the "I" what the latter strives for in its desiring, namely, that it needs to acknowledge nothing other than itself. But the experience which the self-consciousness of desire inevitably has is, after all, that that alone which by self-negation can give it self-consciousness, has to be self-consciousness itself. That means, however, that the second self-consciousness is not only free to voluntarily confirm the self-consciousness of the first, but also to deny recognition of it.[7]

One might well expect, then, that in the process of assuring itself of the recognition which self-consciousness needs, self-consciousness comes to direct its desire to another self-consciousness and seeks to deprive the latter of its independence. And as a matter of fact that is the case: in the self-consciousness of the master this new experience begins—an experience which leads, it must be added, to a higher form of free self-consciousness through the experience of the servant, not that of the master. But, before treating that experience, this famous chapter with the caption, "Independence and Dependence of Self-consciousness: Mastery and Servitude," opens, as do all the others

---

7. Kojève (in the German edition of his lectures, *Hegel,* ed. I. Fetscher, Stuttgart, 1958, pp. 12 ff.) and, following him, Hyppolite (*Etudes sur Marx et Hegel,* Paris, 1955, pp. 181 ff.) even interprets the transition from desire (*Begierde*) to recognized self-consciousness using the concept of desire as a basis. True desire, they say, is the desire of the desire of another (*désir du désir d'un autre*), i.e., love. Hegel himself, however, does not call that *Begierde* any longer, and in point of fact this French description of the transition from *Begierde* to recognized self-consciousness sounds wrong in German. If only Hegel had at least said *Verlangen* (yearning, desire). *Still the French sense of désir* can be detected in certain German expressions, for instance in the word *Ehrbegierde* (desire for honor) which does include the element of *désir*. On the other hand, there is no sense of *désir* in the German *Liebesbegierde* (desire to be loved), which expresses something beyond the carnal human sense which *Begierde* often has. For that reason Kojève's quite nice illustration of the essence of human *Begierde*—that it desires an object, even if it be intrinsically worthless, for the sole reason that somebody else desires it, is not yet apropos at the stage here. That illustration is used too early for it has its true value as an illustration of later stages along Hegel's way, above all, the world of alienated spirit.

with an introduction in which Hegel analyzes the concept of the self-consciousness which has now been reached—a self-consciousness for which another self-consciousness is necessary. Here the dialectic of the concept of recognition is developed, that is for us, for the philosophical analysis which we are applying to this concept.

For us, namely, it is clear that if self-consciousness exists only when recognized as such, it will necessarily get caught up in the dialectic implied in the nature of recognition. Hegel describes the dialectic resulting from the doubling of self-consciousness as that of the "spiritual unity." The word, "spiritual," is carefully chosen here. For we know that there is something like spirit, which is not self-consciousness as an individual point, but rather a "world," which because it is social, lives by reciprocal recognition. Hence at the start, Hegel is considering the dialectic of self-consciousness taken as the movement of recognition as the latter appears to us. We have, in other words, a reflection per se, which is not that of the consciousness in question, but rather that of the concept. Clearly, the concern here is not just with one sort of doubling of consciousness, i.e., with the fact that there is another self-consciousness for self-consciousness. Besides that there is the duplication of self-consciousness within itself, for as self-consciousness which in itself is split and united, it itself says "I" to itself: and in this way it is the inner difference or infinitude which, as self-consciousness, it shares with life. But at this new stage we are concerned with the actualization of this infinitude, with the concept of "infinitude which is being realized in self-consciousness." The inner difference between "I" and "I" lying in self-consciousness now appears, now becomes the real difference of the "we" which is "I" and "you," real "I" and real other "I." That occurs in the movement of recognition.[8] It is a complicated movement, for it does not suffice to say that self-consciousness has lost itself *in* the other or *to* the other, i.e., that it only has its self-consciousness in the other. If this were so, then it would no longer see the other as a self at all, but rather, only "itself" in the other. That would in fact be the case if it were so obsessed with honor that it sought to find its own self-consciousness in the other. And what it would see here is not at all the being of the other, but rather only its own being in otherness, its own being another, in which it believes itself to be confirmed. That, however,

---

8. Gadamer deals extensively with the I-Thou relationship and the phenomenon of recognition within the framework of his hermeneutic theory. Cf. WM 340 ff. (TRANS.)

will not suffice. To be sure, as was the case for desire, self-consciousness must cancel "the other being standing on its own" in order to be certain of itself. But it must also hold itself back out of respect to the other, for this other is itself and it is essential for self-consciousness that the other continue to exist. Its own self-consciousness depends on the other, but the dependence here is unlike that of desire on its object—an object which is simply to be eliminated. Here self-consciousness depends in a more spiritual sense on the other as self. Only if the other is not merely the other of the first self-consciousness, "his other," but rather free precisely in opposition to a self, can it provide confirmation of the first's self-consciousness. That a person demands recognition from another implies, to be sure, that the other is canceled, but on the other hand, what is demanded of the other implies to an equal extent that the other is recognized as free and hence implies just as much the return of the other to itself, to its free existence, as it implies the return of the first self-consciousness to itself. There is not only the confirmation of one's own self here, but also confirmation of the self of the other.

And now it is clear that this whole process is only valid if it is completely reciprocal. Take for instance a trivial form of recognition, the greeting. "Each sees the other doing the same thing it is doing. Each does itself what it demands of the other. And for that reason it does what it does only insofar as the other does the same. One-sided action would serve no purpose . . ." (142). As a matter of fact, it would not only be without purpose: it would be fatal for one's own consciousness of self. Think of the feeling of humiliation when a greeting is not returned, be it because the other refuses to take cognizance of you—a devastating defeat for your own consciousness of self—or because he is not the person you thought he was but someone else and hence does not recognize you—not a very nice feeling either. Reciprocity is that essential here. "They recognize each other as recognizing reciprocally," indeed, "a qualification of many facets and many connotations."

This illustration of the dialectic of recognition using the custom of the greeting is not merely a convincing example for the dialectic on the conceptual level. It is a convincing anticipation of the real social background which lies behind Hegel's description of the experience of self-consciousness and which explains the decisive role he assigns to death in his system. Hegel relies here upon a very concrete experience. The dialectic of recognition is experienced in a process, that is, in the life and death conflict, and in the determination of self-consciousness to prove its truth, its being recognized, even at the risk of its life. That there is a genuine connection of this sort is confirmed in the institution of the duel—two people fighting it out to restore honor which has been offended. He who is ready to fight with the other, he who does another the honor of being willing to fight with him, demonstrates thereby that he did not intend to place the latter beneath him. And, conversely, he who demands satisfaction, demonstrates for his part that he cannot bear the humiliation he has suffered unless the other, by declaring himself ready to fight, nullifies it. As is well known, in a matter of honor, no other form of nullification will suffice, and the one offended may therefore refuse any form of reconciliation. The code of honor admits only the full reciprocity of the life and death conflict, for it alone restores the mutual recognition in which self-consciousness finds its social confirmation. That one would give one's all for one's honor bears witness to the significance of honor. And when Hegel demonstrates in what follows that the confirmation of self-consciousness achieved in being a master cannot be that of true self-consciousness and that the self-consciousness of ability in the slave who works is higher than that of the master who only enjoys, that too is not without confirmation in social practice. The bourgeoisie, which ascends by virtue of its work, takes over the nobility's code of honor, but once it loses its new sense of belonging to the ruling classes, it no longer understands that code. Its imitation of nobility's code of honor as instanced in the "academic" duels for satisfaction fought by "ruling class" students and graduates becomes meaningless. Thus it is historically correct to say that the existence of such a code of honor is the symbolic representation of the result of the life and death conflict in which mastery and servitude split apart. Still, what Hegel provides is an "ideal-type" construction of the relationship of mastery and servitude, which is merely illustrated by the historical background of the emergence of mastery.[9] When Hegel derives free self-consciousness from the essential connection between the absoluteness of freedom and the absoluteness of death, he is not giving us an early history of the development of mastery. Nor is he giving us a

9. Accordingly, the historical question of the origin of mastery as it is explained in contemporary ethnology—as an outgrowth of the conquest of peasant peoples by invading horsemen—can be held in abeyance. That theory is intended to explain how the master-slave structure of the state comes into being. Here, however, where we are still moving completely within the sphere of self-consciousness, that question is not thematic.

history of the liberation from mastery. Rather, he provides an ideal genealogy of the relationship between master and servant.[10]

A self-consciousness which as living self-consciousness merely finds itself together with other self-consciousness, i.e., "independent forms, consciousnesses submerged . . . in the being of life" (143), does not yet have validity. As pure being for itself, i.e., as *self*-consciousness, it must present itself in and stand the test of the life and death conflict. The reciprocity of the code of honor which we described above is perfectly suited to make clear that this "presentation" cannot consist solely in self-consciousness's endeavor to annihilate the other existence, but rather that it must consist also in the elevation of its being above its own particular existence, its "being attached to life" (144). Thus the reason why it must put its own life on the line is not that it is unable to become certain of itself without annihilation of the other and accordingly without a conflict with the other, but rather that it is unable to achieve true being-for-self without overcoming its attachment to life, i.e., without annihilation of itself as mere "life." Only in this annihilation can it become certain of itself. Of course a further insight contradicting this one will come, namely, that the mutual risk of life cannot bring about what it is supposed to: certainty of self. The point of this dialectic is evidenced in the fact that the one who survives is no closer to his goal than the one who succumbs. That which is able to give self-consciousness certainty of itself must be a cancellation of the other self-consciousness different from outright annihilation of the latter. Thus life is not only "as essential as pure self-consciousness" to the one who subjugates himself, but also to the other as well: the latter specifically needs the life of the first, but as a consciousness which is not for itself but for another. Because it has no true being for itself, the consciousness which submits is, like the slave of antiquity, "thing-ness," object, *res.* Thus the result of the experience of the life and death struggle for recognition is indeed

10. Kojève, as his epoch making introduction to Hegel's thought (*Introduction à la Lecture de Hegel,* Paris, 1947) demonstrates, sees this quite clearly. His own way to Hegel, which is determined by the bloodletting of the Russian October Revolution and by the ensuing wish to acquire a better understanding of Marx, led him to apply Hegel historically in ways which are not entirely convincing. This is not the place to refute either the Marxists or Heidegger, even if it remains true that every revolution is bloody, just as is every war. Kojève's work, however, retains its value today, in particular, because it was he who first revealed the philosophic significance of the Jena manuscripts for understanding Hegel's conception of death.

that self-consciousness can only be when it finds itself confirmed in the other. That means, however, that it is double and that it divides into master and servant.

The dialectic of the master and servant is now worked out in two courses of experience: that of the master and that of the servant (148).[11] This exposition presents no special difficulties as far as the master is concerned. It is easy to see that the master achieves satisfaction of his desire with the help and service of the servant. The independence of the things on which the self-consciousness of desire remained dependent is now canceled. The servant delivers the thing, which he has worked on, to the master for the "pure" pleasure of the latter. As Kojève puts it, the servant sets the master's table. Why does the consciousness of the master nevertheless remain a faulty (*verkehrtes*) self-consciousness? One might expect that here Hegel would play upon the master's dependency on the servant. This dependency is well known to us, not only from the Marxist slogan of the "general strike," but also from the dialectic of the will to power as Nietzsche develops it, and as it is confirmed in the everyday experience of serving. There is a dependency of the master on the servant and it demonstrates the falsity of the master's self-consciousness or, so to speak, the latter's actual servitude. Certainly, it stands as a matter of fact that the master becomes dependent on the servant and that the consciousness of being a master finds itself thereby limited. But Hegel's dialectical analysis is far more rigorous. It seeks out the dialectical reversal within the self-consciousness of the master and is not content with a limitation which is externally imposed on mastery. As regards the mere fact of the master's dependency, could one not ask, is it not too bad for the facts that they do not allow the master his full mastery? The master who knows himself to be dependent on his servant no longer has the genuine self-consciousness of a master but that of a servant—a phenomenon which includes, we know, the most comical forms of anxious obedience to the servant. For us it is clear that such a master is no master. But is it clear for the master? Is he not comical precisely because he feels himself to be a master, yet in truth is afraid? We who recognize the dependency of the master know as well that his dependency is actually that of desire and does not come from his failure to be recognized. But a new level of falsity in the self-consciousness of the master which would cause it to collapse would be reached only then when

11. Cf. Ph 148: "We only saw what servitude is in relationship to mastery."

as self-consciousness it knew itself to be inferior to another sort of self-consciousness. The essential point in Hegel's argument seems to me to be that it is aimed precisely at the master's coming to realize his inferiority and that it rejects the more obvious dialectic of dependency. Hegel's argument deals with the consciousness of a master who is and remains a master. He has achieved everything he should—specifically, that another self-consciousness cancels itself as being-for-self and does to itself what the first self-consciousness does to it. Indeed, the servant is not only treated as an object, but also treats himself as an object, i.e., he is absorbed in service and thus has his "self-consciousness" only in the master. In everything he does, the servant faithful to his master has the master in mind and not himself. He makes sure that the thing is nothing to the master and that the master is pure being-for-self, which sees itself confirmed in the services rendered to it. To this extent recognition ought to be achieved here.

But of what value to the master, to his self-consciousness, is the existence of such a servant? Here is Hegel's argument. The most august master, whom the servant never allows to have even the slightest sense of dependency—precisely this "master-only" must recognize that he is thereby not certain of his being-for-self as the truth. What he is certain of in the servant is, after all, the dependency and inessentiality of the servile consciousness. That alone is his "truth" and it is a "faulty truth." Thus Hegel is able to find the dialectical reversal within self-consciousness itself—in its claim, and not in its factual vulnerability. The truth of self-consciousness will have to be sought, not in the consciousness of the master but in the servile consciousness—even if "to begin with," this consciousness is "outside of itself," i.e., knows itself in the master and does not know itself as the truth of self-consciousness, or, does not know that the master is not the "independent consciousness" at all, but rather it itself.

Thus the reversal follows in which servile consciousness as consciousness pushed back into itself, i.e., as consciousness having returned to itself from having been outside itself, withdraws into itself. And like someone who withdraws into himself, it begins to think differently. Or, to put this point in context, it now thinks with new awareness of self. Per se, servitude is the very antithesis of genuine self-consciousness. "For servitude the master is at first the essence." There is implied in the consciousness of serving the complete surrendering of self to the master and his needs. That means the complete subordination of all one's own needs to the sole important thing, service, service to the master who alone is important. Thus for the consciousness of service "independent consciousness which is for itself is . . . the truth," but obviously it is not entirely aware of this. This consciousness does not yet have a self-consciousness or being-for-self of its own. Since servitude is entirely "for the other," the truth of independent consciousness, i.e., that it is itself independent consciousness, exists "for it," but not yet "in it."

And here Hegel once again bases his argument on the role which the life and death conflict played for self-consciousness. He calls death the absolute master, meaning that there is yet a greater master than that into the service of which the servant delivers himself and to which he forfeits his independence. When one accepts the self-surrender of service, the human master too brings one to "dissolve" the ties with one's own natural existence and to deny the exigencies of it. That is implied in the servant's complete self-subordination. Nothing is as important to the consciousness which serves as the contentment of the master. But how much more in the fear of death, that total dissolution, does one in giving up everything outside oneself want to cling to oneself, "the simple self-consciousness, pure being-for-self"! The absolute master, death, which demands absolute subjugation, throws the trembling individual entirely upon himself alone.

At this point, precisely because nothing else which one could hang onto withstands the fear of death, pure being-for-self is raised to the level of consciousness, which is to say that consciousness's actual concern is now for it.[12] And that is the reason why servitude now acquires a self-consciousness of service: the servant proves his own being-for-self to himself in a new way, one different from the self-sacrifice of service: "it [servile consciousness] thereby cancels in each single aspect [i.e., not only in the universal dissolution in the fear of death] its attachment to natural existence and works this off." "Working off natural existence"—a key phrase has been reached here, one which indicates how knowledge of pure being-for-self, which the serving consciousness is now aware of for itself, is realized. Through work. Work is "inhibited desire": instead of immediately satisfying its desire, consciousness keeps to itself and does not annihilate the object ("delayed

---

12. If Gadamer is correct in his interpretation, death has the same role in Hegel's understanding of the transition from consciousness to self-consciousness as it has in Heidegger's understanding of the transition from inauthenticity to authenticity. The higher stage for both Hegel and Heidegger would be *Sein zum Tode,* being towards death, for it is only death which can put the individual in authentic relationship with himself. Cf. SZ 46–53 (TRANS.)

disappearance"). Rather by "shaping" it, imprinting its form upon
it, it converts it into something which remains. In producing the object, consciousness which works comes to "view independent being
as itself." The meaning is clear. We have here the self-consciousness
of ability, which sees itself continually and lastingly confirmed in
that which it "shapes" and has shaped. Through work, self-consciousness which is for-itself settles in the "element of permanency." That,
indeed, is the positive significance of forming: it yields a self-consciousness which even the slave can have. In essence, we have reached
the *eph hēmin* of Stoic consciousness.

Hegel, with ample justification, supplements this line of thought
with a second. For there is a negative side of "forming" which goes
deeper, in that it makes it possible to transcend fear.[13] Only now does
it become completely clear that we are concerned with a phase in the
genealogy of freedom, indeed, the decisive phase. The freedom of
self-consciousness consists not only in the confirmation of self given
in existent things (*seiendes*), but also in successful self-assertion in
opposition to dependency on existent things. In bringing forth the
product of its work, consciousness emerges for itself not as an existent thing, but rather as "being-for-self for itself." Here again Hegel
finds self-consciousness's "trembling before the strange reality" to be
of decisive importance for it. And, as a matter of fact, the mere anxiety of servile existence is by itself not the beginning of freedom. That
someone in the anxiety of conflict places life before honor certainly
does not yet indicate that he has suffered that trembling in the very
innermost fibers of himself, a trembling in which alone one becomes
certain of one's pure "being-for-self." He who in disregarding an of-
fense to honor, i.e., who in spite of the fact that recognition has been
refused him clings to life, is in reality a slave held by the chain of natural existence. Hegel goes so far as to say that someone could "be
recognized as a person even though he himself does not attain the
truth of being recognized as an independent self-consciousness"—a
remarkable statement. Evidently, Hegel is referring to the fact that
the law, which treats no one as a thing (*res*), but rather always requires that the individual be recognized as a person, does not insure

13. It is only in response to a typical misunderstanding (H. Popitz, *Der
entfremdete Mensch,* Basel, 1953, pp. 131 ff.) that I would emphasize that
the "negative" concept of work in Hegel, if taken to be evaluative, is actually
a positive concept, no matter what one's point of view is. For the most part
Hegel tends to use Hegelian concepts like "negative" here in a Hegelian sense.

real self-consciousness precisely because it pronounces judgment "without regard to the person," i.e., in recognition of all persons as equal. The elimination of slavery, then, does not yet end man's sense of being a servant. Work which one no longer performs for a master does not for that reason imply that the individual doing it is made free for true self-consciousness. In fact not even one's "dexterity" put to free use would mean that. It too can represent a freedom which remains at the level of servitude, for such dexterity can be successful at all sorts of things without being independent, consciousness, i.e., as true ability, a self-consciousness of "vocation." Similarly, obstinacy is only thought to confirm freedom and is, in fact, a form of rebellious dependency.

In contrast, if work is to be the basis of true self-consciousness, it must derive from what I have termed above "consciousness of ability," something which is able to deal with the "universal might [death] and objective reality" (150). Hegel further develops this idea of freedom of ability by emphasizing that the formative activity cancels opposed, existent form. "But this objective, negative reality is precisely the alien reality before which it trembled." That is a daring thesis, and it remains for us to explicate it. Unquestionably, the experience of death is the experience of an ultimate dependency in our existence, which the latter in its being-for-self immediately resists. This alien master, who is master over everything, thus stands for everything alien on which our own self-consciousness is dependent. In this sense every cancellation of such an alien reality—and even if it be only a skilled cancellation of the existent form of things—is a liberation of our own self-consciousness. Only in this is there contained the confirmation proper to the self-consciousness of ability, namely, that it comes to be "for it as its own," this not only in the single existent which it produces, but beyond this, in its own being-for-self as ability. "It posits itself"; it establishes itself as being-for-self in the element of permanency and is no longer mere dissolution in natural existence which "works off" its trembling with the feeling of self characteristic of anxiety and service. Although in work for the master it seemed to have no mind of its own (and as service did indeed have none), consciousness which serves, in surrendering itself to work as work—and not simply to the master—becomes conscious of itself. When it "puts out" the form as its own (when it produces), it recognizes itself. And thus precisely in work it has a mind of its own: "That, I can do!" To be sure, this is not yet the full encounter with self which, for instance, the work of art affords and which allows us to recognize, "That's me!"

Hegel is not worried about the specific form which working consciousness has given the thing and which would allow consciousness to recognize itself in it. Indeed, his concern is not at all with the "thing," but
rather only with form *qua* form. The sole thing which confirms self-
consciousness here is the fact that the form is one which it itself gives
to the thing and that it is one and the same each time. Thus self-con-
firmation is not achieved in viewing any particular existent as such,
but only in the form which is one's own and which precisely for this
reason brings out the pure being-for-self contained in the freedom of
one's ability. Therefore, strictly speaking, it is not at all the ability as
such, this "dexterity," which withstands total dissolution—annihilation
by the "not" of otherness—and provides the basis for true self-consciousness, but rather the consciousness of one's ability.

The history of freedom has by no means come to an end here, but
in the history of the consciousness of freedom the decisive step has
been taken. That is demonstrated by what follows: as the "total dissolution" of self-consciousness, this being-for-self has become "a new
form of self-consciousness, a consciousness which *thinks,* i.e., a consciousness which is free self-consciousness" (151). What we have here
is something truly universal in which you and I are the same. It will
be developed as the self-consciousness of reason. Indeed, having reason or exhibiting reasonableness means being able, in disregard of
oneself, to accept as valid that in which no single self can consider
himself superior to another. That two times two equals four is not
my truth, not your truth and not a truth in need of mutual recognition by each of us. It is reason as certainty of being all reality. Since
now the "other" cannot be other than reason, a firm basis is established here for experience, for the standpoint of observing reason.
But beyond this, it is particularly true for all actualization or realization of self-consciousness, i.e., for all active reason, that the objective, real world "has lost every sense of being alien" (314).[14] Here
we have reached spirit, i.e., spirit in the form of genuine universality
such as ethicality and custom, which in being taken for granted,
unite one and all. Self-consciousness is not lost in this universality.
Rather it finds itself there and to its satisfaction, it knows its single-
ness was wrong.

---

14. Observing Reason (*Beobachtende Vernunft*) and the Realization of Self-
consciousness (*Verwirklichung des Selbstbewusstseins*) are two consecutive
stages in Hegel's *Phenomenology of Mind.* Cf. Ph 183 ff. and Ph 255 ff.
(TRANS.)

It has not helped in understanding this chapter that Karl Marx made use of its master-servant dialectic in a very different context. As we have shown above Marx does not simply misunderstand and misuse Hegel, for it is true that through work the servant reaches a higher.self-consciousness than the master who enjoys; and that, indeed, is the presupposition of the former's liberation from servitude in the external realm of his social existence—as it was for the bourgeois citizen before him.

However, Hegel, in his dialectic, does not describe the wage worker, but principally the farmer and handworker in bondage. The emancipation of the cities and then of the farmers as it occurs in the revolutionary ascent of the *tiers état* to a position of political respon-sibility, is only similar in structure to the liberation of capitalism's wage-slave. In point of fact, for self-consciousness the actual purpose of work is fulfilled in the non-alienated work world. In the "phenome-nology of spirit" which Hegel describes, the inner freedom of self-con-sciousness which results from the dialectic of mastery and servitude is by no means the last word. Accordingly, the critical approach which seeks, and then fails to find the liberation of the wage-slave from the mastery of capital in the result of Hegel's dialectic, is quite superficial. As an argument against the man who taught the unity of the "real" and the "reasonable"—and that, incidentally, can most certainly not mean the approbation of things as they stand—one cannot propose, as an updated critical insight, that self-consciousness, as free, must work itself into the whole of objective reality, that it must reach the self-evident truth of the solidarity of ethical spirit and the community of ethical customs, that it must complete the actualization of reason as a human and social task. Marx, to be sure, found the point at which to apply his criticism of Hegel not here, but rather, as seemed more appropriate, in Hegel's philosophy of right. But the dogmatic concep-tion of consciousness and of idealism which he shared with his con-temporaries kept him from recognizing that Hegel would never have dreamt for a moment that work is only the work of thought and that what is reasonable would be realized solely through thought. Thus the work of which Hegel speaks is material work too, and the experi-ence consciousness has is that all handwork is a matter of the spirit. Now let us assume that it is true that the mode of production in mod-ern industry and the form of human commerce in the industrial society do not permit the worker to find a significance for himself in his work, which alone would make self-consciousness possible. Then, in view of the comprehensive character of this mode of work, the question necessarily arises who could be really free in the industrial society of to-day with its ubiquitous coercion of things and pressure to consume. Precisely in regard to this question Hegel's dialectic of master and servant seems to delineate a valid truth: if there is to be freedom, then first of all the chain attaching us to things must be broken. The path of mankind to universal prosperity is not as such the path to the freedom of all. Just as easily, it could be a path to the unfreedom of all.

4

The Idea of Hegel's Logic

Surprisingly, in our century Hegel's philosophy has returned to favor after decades of playing the role of whipping boy and representing the quintessence of that "speculative" philosophy held in contempt by those oriented towards the empirical sciences. Even today such an opinion of his thought prevails in the Anglo-Saxon world. Interest in Hegel first gradually revived during the era of neo-Kantianism. At the turn of the century, there were impressive advocates of speculative idealism in Italy and Holland, England and France; to mention only a few, Croce, Bolland, and Bradley. At the same time the Hegelianism latently at work in neo-Kantianism emerged in the philosophic consciousness of the time in Germany, above all in William Windelband's Heidelberg circle (to which men like Julius Ebbinghaus, Richard Kroner, Paul Hensel, George Lukács, Ernst Bloch, and others belonged) and also in the continuing development of the Marburg school (Nicolai Hartmann, Ernst Cassirer). Still Hegel's philosophy had no real presence here since it sufficed for this so-called neo-Hegelianism to merely reiterate Hegel's criticism of Kant.

But that was changed in Germany by the impulse coming from Martin Heidegger and, after that, by the interest of French social scientists in Hegel which was awakened above all by the lectures of Alexander Kojève. Both of these initiatives aroused a rather one-sided philosophic interest in Hegel's first great work, the *Phenomenology of Spirit*. The *Logic*, in contrast, remained till today very much in the background. As a matter of fact, however, the *Phenomenology of Spirit* is not the main systematic work of the Hegelian philosophy which prevailed through decades of the nineteenth century. Indeed, the *Phenomenology of Spirit* is a kind of anticipation of what was to come in which Hegel tried to summarize the whole of his philosophy from a certain point of view. As opposed to Kant, the author of the three "critiques," who found himself arguing about their function with those who followed him, there was no doubt for Hegel that this phenomenological introduction to his system was in no sense the system of philosophic sciences itself. In contrast, the *Science of Logic* is not merely a first step in the direction of constructing the system of philosophic sciences, as the so-called *Encyclopedia* was later to present it, rather it is the first part of that system and its foundation. Moreover, the *Encyclopedia of Philosophic Sciences* is itself actually only a textbook for Hegel's lectures, these being the source of his great influence on the nineteenth century—for this influence stemmed not so much from the sibylline depth of his books as from his extraordinary ability to make his listeners perceive his meaning. Basically, Hegel's only books are the *Phenomenology of Spirit* and the *Science of Logic,* the sole part of his system which he actually completed. Even Hegel's most famous published book, to which the nineteenth century turned above all his others, his *Philosophy of Right,* is in truth nothing but a textbook for academic instruction and not the actual elaboration of a part of the system. All these facts indicate that it is time to place the *Science of Logic* closer to the center of Hegel research than it has been heretofore and my hope is that an understanding of Hegel's idea of the science of logic might show the way for coming to grips with it which our present philosophic interests demand.

To begin with, I shall treat the idea of Hegel's *Logic* generally. I shall proceed then to the method of this *Logic.* Thirdly, I will examine somewhat more precisely the starting point of the *Logic,* one of the most discussed problems of Hegel's philosophy. In conclusion, I shall discuss the relevance of Hegel's *Logic,* above all in reference to its bearing on the problem of language which plays such a central role in the philosophy of today.

With his *Logic* Hegel seeks to bring the transcendental philosophy initiated by Kant to its conclusion. According to Hegel, Fichte was the first to grasp the universal systematic implications of Kant's way of viewing things from the perspective of transcendental philosophy. At the same time, however, Hegel was of the opinion that Fichte's own "Doctrine of Science" did not really finish the task of developing the entirety of human knowledge out of self-consciousness. To be sure, Fichte's contention is that his "Doctrine of Science" had done precisely that. He saw, in the spontaneity of self-consciousness, the actual, underlying operation, "the active deed" (*Tathandlung*), as he calls it. This autonomous deed of self-consciousness, i.e., its determining itself in relation to itself, which Kant had formulated in the

concept of autonomy as the essence of practical reason, was now to
be the point of origin for every truth of human knowledge. The "I"
is this "immediate self-consciousness" (L I 61). Hegel's objection is
that here the ideal of a pure "I" as self-consciousness is insisted upon
from the start, without the process of mediation which should lead
up to it. Such a subjective supposition as this, he argues, does not in
the least guarantee a sure understanding of what the self, i.e., the "I"
in the transcendental sense, might be.

Now one must resist simply accepting Hegel's version of this state
of affairs, according to which Fichte taught a merely subjective idealism, Hegel himself being the first to join this subjective idealism with
the objective idealism of Schelling's philosophy of nature in the
grand, authentic synthesis of absolute idealism. In point of fact,
Fichte's "Doctrine of Science" depends very much upon the idea of
absolute idealism, i.e., on the development of the entire content of
knowledge as the complete whole of self-consciousness. Nevertheless
one must concede to Hegel that Fichte, instead of really completing
the introduction into the standpoint of the "Doctrine of Science"—
that is, the elevation and purification of the empirical "I" to the
transcendental "I"—actually only insisted upon it. Precisely this elevation is what Hegel now claims to have accomplished through his
Phenomenology of Spirit. One can also express the matter as follows:
Hegel demonstrates that the pure "I" is spirit. That is the result which
spirit reaches at the end of its course of appearances. It leaves behind
its appearance as consciousness and as self-consciousness (including
the "recognized" self-consciousness of the "we") as well as all forms
of reason and spirit which still contain the opposition of consciousness and its object. The truth of the "I" is pure knowing. Thus, at the
end of the *Phenomenology*'s final chapter on "absolute knowing"
stands the idea of a philosophical science whose *moments* are no
longer determinate forms of consciousness, but rather determinate
concepts. In its initial form such a science must be the science of
logic. The beginning of science is therefore based upon the result of
consciousness's experience, which commences with "Sense Certainty" and is completed in the forms of spirit which Hegel calls "absolute knowing": "art," "religion" and "philosophy." They are absolute because they are no longer opinions of consciousness which extend to an object beyond that which presents and fully affirms itself
within these forms. Science first begins here, because here for the
first time nothing but thoughts, that is nothing but the pure concept,

is thought in its determinacy (Ph 562). Absolute knowing is thus the result of a purification in the sense that the truth of Fichte's concept of the transcendental "I" emerges, not merely as being a subject, but rather as reason and spirit and, accordingly, as all of reality. Thus Hegel lays his very own foundation, on which he rebuilds absolute knowing as the truth of metaphysics as Aristotle, for one, conceived of it in *nous* or Aquinas, for another, in *intellectus agens.* And thus a universal logic—which explicates the ideas of God before the creation—is made possible. Hegel's concept of spirit which transcends the subjective forms of self-consciousness thus goes back to the *logos-nous* metaphysics of the Platonic and Aristotelian tradition, which predates the whole question of self-consciousness. In this fashion, Hegel achieves his objective of reinstating the Greek *logos* on the new foundation of modern, self-knowing spirit. The light in which all truth is seen is cast from consciousness's becoming clear about itself. No other, no further ontological or theological justification is given.

If one wishes to characterize the idea of Hegel's logic from this viewpoint, a comparison with Plato's dialectic is useful, for that is the model which Hegel always has in mind. In Greek philosophy Hegel saw the philosophy of *logos,* or put another way, the courage to consider pure thoughts per se. As a result, Greek thought succeeded in unfolding the universe of ideas. For this realm Hegel coins a new expression, typical of him, but which I have yet to find in anyone before him, namely, "the logical." What he is characterizing here is the entire cosmos of ideas as Plato's philosophy dialectically develops it. Now Plato was driven by the desire to provide justification for every thought and his doctrine of ideas was intended to satisfy the demand which Socrates makes in the dialogues that for every contention a reason or argument must always be given (*logon didonai*). For his part, Hegel will claim that his dialectic in the *Logic* meets the requirement of accounting for the rightness of each individual thought by explicating them all within a system. Of course, such an "account" as that could not be given in live, Socratic dialogue, where each successive stage of presumed knowledge is abandoned as the participants proceed through a sequence of questions and answers and then finally come to an understanding.[1] Nor could it be given by grounding this procedure, as Plato did, in the doctrine of ideas. Rather, the basis has

1. Gadamer's earliest published book, *Platos Dialektische Ethik,* thematizes the Socratic technique of guiding discussion. Cf. in particular section 2, "Das Gespräch und der *Logos,*" pp. 22 ff., and section 5, "Der Sokratische Dialog," pp. 40 ff. (TRANS.)

to be the methodologically rigorous one of a "science" which ultimately is founded upon Descartes's idea of method and which, within
the framework of transcendental philosophy, is developed from the
principle of self-consciousness. The systematic derivation of pure
concepts in the *Science of Logic,* in which spirit has attained "the
pure.element of its existence, i.e., the concept," subsequently determines the system of science as a whole. That derivation presents the
universe of possible thought as the necessity governing the continuing
self-determination of the concept. The objective of this exposition is
such that Plato's unending discussion of the soul with itself could
only serve as a formal model.

A glance back at Greek philosophy is necessary, too, if one is to understand Hegel's conception of the method through which he sought
to convert traditional logic into a genuine philosophical science—the
method of dialectic. Dialectic develops from the magnificent bold-
ness of the Eleatics, who, in opposition to what appears to be the
case in sense experience, held strictly and relentlessly to what thought
and thought alone demands. It is a well known observation of Hegel's
that these Greek thinkers were the first to leave firm ground and to
risk the high seas of thinking solely with the aid of thought itself.
They were the first to demand and to carry out that pure thinking to
which the title of as recent a work as Kant's *Critique of Pure Reason*
still implicitly refers. The expression, "pure thinking," obviously
points to a Pythagorean-Platonic source. Implied is the purification
or catharsis in which thought is freed from the cloudiness of sense
perception.

Plato portrayed this art of pure thinking in his dramatization of
Socrates' discussions in which the logical consequences of each
thought are pursued unerringly. But Hegel comments with a measure
of justification that Plato's dialectic is deficient in that it is only negative and does not reach any scientific insight. As a matter of fact,
Plato's dialectic is, properly speaking, not a method at all and least of
all the transcendental method of Fichte or Hegel. It has no absolute
beginning. Nor is it founded on an ideal of absolute knowledge which
could be said to be free from all opposition between knowing and
what is known and be held to embrace all knowledge in such a way
that the entire content of knowledge would be exhausted in the continuing determination of the concept in relationship to itself. For
Hegel something else was paradigmatic in Plato, namely, the concat-
enation of ideas. Plato's underlying conviction, which we find

developed above all in the *Parmenides,* is that there is no truth of a
single idea and, accordingly, that isolating an idea always means missing the truth. Ideas exist only linked, mixed, or interwoven as they
are encountered in discussion or are "there" each time in the discourse of the soul with itself. Human thought is not constituted like
an originative, infinite, on looking mind. Rather, it can only grasp
what is, in discursive development of its thoughts. Kant, for one,
also brought this point into sharp relief by limiting legitimate concepts to those which refer to experience. But be that as it may, the
truth visible behind Plato's *Parmenides* was that the *logos* is always a
complex of ideas, i.e., the relationship of ideas to each other. And to
this extent the first truth of Hegel's *Logic* is a Platonic one which is
to be perceived even in the *Meno,* when it is said that all of nature is
interrelated and that therefore the path of recollection of one thing
is the path of recollection of all things. There are no single ideas, and
it is the purpose of dialectic to dispel the untruth of their separateness.

That is most easily seen in regard to the determinations of "reflection."[2] Everyone knows that identity would have no meaning by itself if self-sameness and differentness were not implied in it. Identity
without difference would be absolutely nothing. Thus the determinations of reflection provide a most convincing argument for the internal linkage of ideas with each other. As a matter of fact, these determinations are the basis of the argument in the *Sophist* since they are
prerequisite for any interweaving of ideas into a unified whole of discussion. Now to be sure, one must keep in mind that even in Plato's
dialectic of ideas the pure concepts of reflection which properly belong to the *logos* are not distinguished from "world concepts" with
complete clarity. Thus in the *Sophist* just as in the *Timaeus* cosmo-
logical concepts like motion and rest are fused in a curious way with
the concepts of reflection, difference, and self-sameness. This fusion
is the basis of Hegel's claim that dialectic makes the entirety of ideas
thinkable. At the same time, the fundamental distinction in Plato between "categories corresponding to the polycombinable vowels of reality," as the *Sophist* puts it, and concepts with content, articulating
a finite region of reality, remains unchallenged. In spite of this,
Hegel's thesis rests on the assumption of unity here. For him objective concepts and concepts of reflection are only different stages of
the same development. The concepts of "being" and the concepts of

2. Cf. L II 23, "die Reflexionsbestimmungen." (TRANS.)

"essence" are completed in the doctrine of the "concept." Consequently what is realized there is a unity of thought and being which corresponds to Aristotle's conception of the category, on the one hand, just as much as it does to Kant's, on the other. The category is the basis of the idea of the new science of logic which Hegel expressly opposes to the traditional form of logic. As he puts it, after Kant had reached the standpoint of transcendental philosophy and taught us to think the *logos* of what is an object, i.e., its categorial constitution, logic could no longer remain formal logic limiting itself to the formal relationship of concept, judgment, and syllogism.

Hegel seeks to give logic a new scientific character by developing the universal system of the concepts of the understanding into a "whole" of science. His starting point is Kant's traditional theory. But while Hegel's system of categories is drawn from thought's reflecting upon itself, the categories are nevertheless no mere determinations of reflection. Kant himself, as a matter of fact, went so far as to call the determinations of reflection "amphibolic" and he excluded them from his table of categories because they have an equivocal function in the determination of objects. Categories are not simply formal determinations of statements or thinking. Rather, they claim to grasp the order of reality in the form of a statement. That is the case in Aristotle, and Kant, for his part, in his theory of synthetic judgments a priori also seeks to explain why pure concepts of the understanding can be legitimately applied to experience of the world given in space and time. Now Hegel's conception of logic would unify this traditional doctrine of categories as the basic concepts of reality constituting the objects of the understanding with the pure determinations of reflection, which are the merely formal determinations of thought. Put another way, he attempts to restore the original objective function of the concept of "form," which it had at first in Aristotle's metaphysics. It is in this way that Hegel's logic, which synthesizes the doctrine of Being and the doctrine of Essence in the doctrine of Concept, is to be understood. The doctrine of Being follows Kant's table of categories insofar as it includes quality and quantity. The doctrine of Essence and the doctrine of the Concept, on the other hand, explicate the categories of relation and modality. All of these possible determinations are now to be systematically derived within the turbulence of continual self-canceling negativity.

The ideal of a science of logic which is to be brought to perfection in this way does not imply that such perfection might ever be completely attained by any individual. Hegel himself fully acknowledges that his own logic is a first attempt which lacks ultimate perfection. What he means, obviously, is that by pursuing multiple paths of derivation, one could work out, as he himself did in his teaching, the fine distinctions of what had only been given in outline form in the *Logic*. Hence, the methodological necessity in the interconnection of concepts as they unfold according to their specific dialectic, is not necessity in the absolute sense. Indeed, one can discern, not only in the second printing of the first volume of the *Logic* as contrasted with the first, but also within one and the same text, that Hegel corrects himself even in his publications. He can say, for instance, that he wishes to present the same subject matter from another point of view, that one can arrive at the same result in another way, etc. Thus Hegel's point is not only that in his *Logic* he did not complete the enormous task before him, but beyond that, in an absolute sense, that it cannot be completed.

It follows from this that a distinction must be made between the concepts as they operate in thought and the thematization of them. It is clear, for example, that one must always use the categories of Essence, e.g., the determinations of Reflection, if one wants to make any statement at all. One cannot utter a sentence without bringing the categories of identity and difference into play. Still, Hegel does not begin his *Logic* with these categories and it would have been of no help to him to do so. Even if he had decided to develop these categories right at the beginning, he would have had to presuppose both. Whoever makes statements uses different words and understands each word to mean this and not that. Both categories, identity and difference, are thereby already implied. The purpose Hegel has in mind for his system thus makes it necessary for him to resort to another construction. In the effort to derive the interrelationship of all categories from each other, a criterion is given in their determinacy per se. All categories are determinations of the content of knowledge, i.e., of the Concept. Since the content must be developed in its manifold determinations in order to arrive at the truth of the Concept, science must begin where there is the least determinacy. In that lies the criterion governing the construction of the *Logic:* there is to be steady advance from the most general (i.e., the least determinate) in which, in a manner of speaking, almost nothing is conceived of, to the full content of the Concept. The entire content of thinking is to be developed in this way.

In more precisely characterizing the idea of the *Logic,* it is necessary too that we be fully conscious of the difference between its method and that of the *Phenomenology of Spirit.* In the introduction to the *Logic,* Hegel himself cites the dialectic of the *Phenomenology* as a first example of his dialectical method. Thus, there is certainly no ultimate difference between the dialectic present in the *Phenomenology* and that in the *Logic.* The belief, based on the subsequent *Encyclopedia,* that phenomenological dialectic did not yet represent the pure method of dialectic, is thus untenable. For one thing, that is demonstrated by the fact that in the preface to the *Phenomenology,* Hegel, in characterizing its dialectical method as the scientific method, uses examples from the *Logic.* As a matter of fact, this preface was written as an introduction to a system which was to consist of two parts: a "Phenomenology of Spirit" and a "Logic and Metaphysics." Nevertheless, there are differences of which one must be aware if one is to grasp to what extent the *Phenomenology of Spirit* is also a science, i.e., to what extent development of its sequence of phenomena can be called a necessary one. In each case the method of dialectic must guarantee that the explication of the train of thought is not arbitrary, that there is no subjective intervention in its development, that there are no transitions from one point to the next which one "selects" on one's own from different perspectives and which, therefore, remain external to the subject matter. On the contrary, the advance from one thought to the next, from one form of knowing to the next, must derive from an immanent necessity. In the *Phenomenology of Spirit* that advance is played out in a most intricate fashion.

The chapters in the dialectic of the *Phenomenology* are so constructed that, as a rule, the dialectical contradictions are first developed out of the concept which is being thematized at that particular moment, e.g., out of the concept of Sense Certainty or Perception. Hence, the first development is of the concepts, as they are "for us" in our reflection about them. Only then is the dialectic described which the consciousness itself experiences and which forces it to change as it changes its opinion of its object. For example, in thinking the sense certainty which fills it, consciousness can no longer believe itself to be thinking anything other than a "universal 'this,'" and thus it must grant that what it meant is a "universal," and that it perceives it as a "thing." It is true that that which proved to be the truth of the old way of knowing is like a new form of knowledge, which believes in a new object. But it comes as something of a surprise to learn, for example, that the "universal this" is the concrete "thing" and the certainty, that of perception. The dialectic of the thing and its properties, in which consciousness is now about to get caught, looks like a new hypothesis which is richer in content and not a necessary consequence of what went before. Still, it appears to me that we are expecting too much here. The dialectic of the new form of knowing, e.g., of perception of the thing, in which the implicit contradictions are exposed, has the appearance of being an arbitrary hypothesis. However, the scientific rigor of the *Phenomenology* is not to be judged by that appearance. On the contrary, this dialectic which we spin out in our reflection is only an ancillary mediation performed on the natural presuppositions of consciousness, one which Hegel works in throughout the text. In contrast to it, the "experience" which the consciousness itself has and which we observe and comprehend, is the proper object of the phenomenological science. Only here does the immanent negativity of the concept develop, which drives the latter to self-sublimation and further determinations of itself. In this there is the necessity of "science," and it is the same in the *Phenomenology* as it is in the *Logic*.

In the *Phenomenology* this scientific advance occurs as a movement back and forth between that which our consciousness believes and that which is actually implied in what it says. Thus, we always find a contradiction between what we want to say and what we actually have said. We are continuously compelled to abandon what proved insufficient and to again set about saying what we mean. Herein consists the method of the *Phenomenology* by which it progresses to its goal, namely to the insight that knowledge properly exists only where that which we believe and that which is are no longer different in any way.

In the *Logic*, on the other hand, there is no place at all allowed for belief. Here knowing is no longer different from its content. Indeed, the conclusion reached in the *Phenomenology* was precisely that the highest form of knowing is that in which there is no longer a difference between belief and what is believed. The first convincing demonstration that "I" and "thing" are the same is provided by the work of art. The work of art is no longer a "thing" which needs to be put into relationship with something beyond itself in order to be comprehended; rather, it makes a "statement," as we say, i.e., it itself dictates how it is to be comprehended. The science of philosophy presupposes the same standpoint of "absolute" knowledge. Accordingly, in the foundation provided for it in its first part, i.e., in the "logic" as the science of possible modes of being, we are concerned with the pure content of thoughts, with thoughts freed from any subjective

opinionation of the one who thinks them. Nothing mystical is intended here. Rather, the knowing in art, religion, and philosophy is
common to all who think, so that in regard to it, it no longer makes
any sense to differentiate one individual consciousness from another.
The forms of the subject's certainty given in the statements of art,
religion, and philosophy, where the reservations of private belief no
longer obtain, are therefore the highest shape spirit assumes. For the
universality of reason consists precisely in its being free of any subjective one-sidedness.

If then private subjectivity is no longer to have a place in the *Logic*,
the question might arise in attempting to understand the dialectic of
the latter, how a movement of concepts can develop there where no
more movement of thought is experienced. Why is the system of concepts something in motion and moving itself and not something
which thought merely runs through?

In the *Phenomenology* the course and goal of the movement of
thought is clear. The movement there is the experience of human
consciousness as it presents itself to the thinking observer. It cannot
maintain its first assumptions, e.g., that sense certainty is the truth,
and is driven from one shape to the next, from consciousness to the
highest objective forms of spirit and ultimately to the forms of absolute spirit in which "you and I are the same soul." But where should
motion begin and where should a path be traversed in the *Logic*,
where the sole concern is with the content of thought and not at all
with its movement? That, precisely, is the problem of the *Logic* and,
in fact, the most discussed point in Hegel's entire systematic project.
Even during his lifetime his opponents—the first and foremost of
which was Schelling—raised the question of how in the *Logic* a movement of ideas could begin and then continue. I would like to show
that this apparent difficulty arises only when one does not adhere
strictly enough to the perspective of reflection in terms of which
Hegel conceives of his transcendental logic.

In this regard, a reference to Plato's *Parmenides* is useful. There too
we are drawn into a movement of thought, though, to be sure, it
seems rather more like the agitation of enthusiasm or of "logical" in-
toxication than a systematic movement towards a goal. There too it
happens to thought, so to speak, that each concept calls for another.
None stays by itself, but rather each ties itself in with another, and
ultimately a contradiction emerges. In this fashion the *Parmenides*
achieves its goal, namely the demonstration that thinking an idea in
isolation is impossible. Something definite can only be thought of

within a context of ideas, which implies, to be sure, that its opposite can also be thought with equal legitimacy. Certainly there is nothing here of Hegel's method. What we do have is more a kind of permanent turbulence since no idea can be valid by itself and since the contradictory result at which thought inevitably arrives calls forth new hypotheses. Still, there is something "systematic" implied here too since the One, which reality is, is developed in the Many which the thought of it contains. It is "systematic" too in that the whole of it unrolls as though it were a dialectical interplay unfolding the extremes of the universal interconnectedness of the ideas, on the one hand, and, on the other, of their separation. Finally, it is "systematic" in the sense that a field of possible determinate knowledge is marked off.

What Hegel claims for his logic, however, is methodologically much more rigorous. Here there is no series of hypotheses which having been merely proposed, are, one after the other, reduced to inconsistency within the complex of ideas. In the *Logic* a starting point is firmly established and then a methodological procedure entered upon in which the knowing subject no longer intrudes. But how do things such as movement and progress commence in this construction of logical thought? That will have to be demonstrated using the beginning of the *Logic*.

To be sure, in taking this route, we must keep in mind that that which can properly be called Hegel's text is the same sort of thing referred to in the philosophy of the Middle Ages as a *corpus*. Hegel insisted repeatedly that introductions, comments, critical excursuses, etc., do not have the same legitimacy as the text, i.e., the course itself of the developing thought. Thus he treats his own introductions—and in the case of the *Logic*, which we are accustomed to read in the second edition, there are no less than four of these at the beginning—as things which do not yet have to do with the subject matter itself. They are concerned solely with the needs of external reflection, that is with relating the material to the conceptions which the reader, whom Hegel's comments are meant to serve, already brings with him. The actual beginning of the *Logic* consists of only a few lines, which, nevertheless, pose the essential problems of Hegelian logic: the beginning with the idea of Being, the identity of it with Nothing, and the synthesis of the two opposed ideas of Being and Nothing, called Becoming. According to Hegel, that constitutes the content of that with which science must begin.

The question of how movement gets into the *Logic* must be

answered in reference to this beginning. Now it is clear, and Hegel makes use of the fact in his commentary, that it lies in the nature of any beginning to be dialectical. Nothing may be presupposed in it and it clearly reveals itself as primary and immediate. But it still is a beginning only if it begins a development, and thus it is determined as a beginning in reference to that development, which is to say that it is "mediated" by the latter. Now let us assume that Being is to be the indeterminate, immediate beginning of the *Logic*. Though it might be evident right away that a Being so abstract "is nothing," how is it to be made evident that from this Being and Nothing a movement to to Becoming develops? How, in the first place, does the movement of the dialectic get started from Being? Though it is convincing that one cannot think Becoming without thinking Being and Nothing simultaneously, the converse, that when one thinks Being and Nothing one must think Becoming is not at all convincing. A transition is made, Hegel claims, but it plainly lacks the evidentness that would allow one to recognize it as dialectically necessary. In contrast, it is very easy to see, for example, that one must progress from the thought of Becoming to the thought of Existence. All becoming is a becoming of something which exists as a result of having become. That is an ancient truth, one already formulated by Plato in the *Philebus* as the *gegennēmenē ousia* or *genesis eis ousian*, respectively. It lies in the very meaning of Becoming itself that it reaches determinacy in that which finally has become. Becoming thus leads to Existence. The transition from Being and Nothing to Becoming is, however, entirely different. Is there a dialectical transition here in the same sense? Hegel himself seems to single out this case as a special one when he comments that Being and Nothing "are only different in belief." That would mean that if both were purely thought by themselves neither would be distinguishable from the other. Thus the pure thought of Being and the pure thought of Nothing would be so little different that their synthesis could not be a new, richer truth of thought. One way Hegel puts this is to say that Nothing "bursts forth immediately" from Being (L I 85). Clearly, the expression, "bursts forth," is one carefully chosen to exclude any idea of mediation and transition. In accord with this it is said on page 79 that talk of such a transition implies the false appearance of separateness. And only in the case of the transition from Being and Nothing to Becoming does Hegel say that "that passing from one to the other does not yet constitute a relationship" (p. 90). Thus that Nothing "bursts forth" from Being is intended to mean that although in our belief Being and Nothing appear as the most extreme opposites, thought cannot succeed in maintaining a distinction here.

Now it is striking that Hegel speaks here of belief (*Meinen*), for distinguishing between belief and what is actually implied in what is said by the holder of that belief, does not properly belong to the themes of the logic of "pure thought" or, as stated on page 78, "is not in the sequence of this exposition. . . ." The *Logic* is concerned with what is present within thought as "content" and develops the determinations of thought as it thinks this presence. Here nothing of the *Phenomenology*'s juxtaposition of belief and what is believed remains. As a matter of fact, the pure thinking of the *Logic* presupposes the result of the dialectic in the *Phenomenology* and thus the subject matter of the *Logic* obviously cannot include belief. Of course, that does not mean that thinking could ever exist without beliefs. It is only meant to imply that between what is believed and what is actually thought and stated no difference at all exists any more. It is now a matter of indifference whether I believe or state something or someone else does. In thinking, that which is held in common is thought, that which excludes all private belief. " 'I' is purified of itself" (p. 60).

Thus if there is recourse to belief at the beginning of the *Logic* that is only because we are still at the level of incipient thought, or, put another way, because as long as we stay at the level of Being and Nothing as what is indeterminate, determination, i.e., thought, has not yet begun. For that reason the difference between Being and Nothing is limited to belief.

Implied in this, however, is that the progression to Becoming cannot be taken as a development in dialectical determination. If, as thought now determines, the difference of Being and Nothing is at the same time their complete lack of difference, then the question how Becoming emerges out of Being and Nothing no longer makes any sense at all. For such a question would certainly imply that there was a thinking which, in a manner of speaking, had not begun to think. Taken as thoughts for thinking, Being and Nothing are not at all determinations of thought. Accordingly, Hegel states explicitly that Being is empty intuition or empty thought per se and that the same holds for Nothing. "Empty" does not mean that something is not, but rather that something is which does not contain what actually ought to be there, something deprived of what it could be. Thus, according to Hegel, light and darkness are two emptinesses to the extent that the complete content of the world consists of things which stand in the light and which eclipse each other. Empty thinking is thus thinking which is not yet that which thinking is at all. And, as a matter of fact, in this way the merging together of Being and Nothing in Becoming can easily be seen to be the proper truth for thought. Thus, saying that "Being passes into Nothing and Nothing passes into Being," is actually a quite untenable way of putting the matter, because a Being already present and distinct from Nothing would thereby be presupposed. If one reads Hegel precisely, one will see that in fact he never speaks of such a transition at all. Instead he says that "what the truth is, is neither Being nor Nothing, but on the contrary, that Being does not now pass over into Nothing nor Nothing into Being, but rather has already passed over"—a transition, accordingly, which has always taken place already. Being and Nothing exist solely as passing over or transition itself, as Becoming. It seems to me most significant that Hegel is able to describe Being and Nothing starting with either intuition or thought (insofar as intuition or thought can be spoken of here). The difference between intuition or thought is itself an empty one as long as nothing determinate is given as content.

Thus Being and Nothing are more to be treated as analytic moments in the concept of Becoming—but "analytic" here neither in the sense of an external reflection, which breaks down the unity of thought by pointing up multiple respects in it, nor in the sense which would imply that out of every synthesis the immanent contradiction can be recovered through analysis of the moments synthesized therein. Such an opposition presupposes things that are different. However, by virtue of their undifferentiatedness, Being and Nothing are only different in the pure and full content of the concept of Becoming.

Hegel's meaning here becomes completely clear when we see how he examines the aspects of Becoming, i.e., "coming-into-being" and "passing-away." It is plain that in this examination the concept of Becoming will be more specifically determined insofar as Becoming now is a coming-to-be or a becoming-nothing. That is to say, Becoming is now determined as transition to something. It is semantically misleading, however, to think of this first determination of Becoming while presupposing the difference of Being and Nothing. In effect that would be to start with the determinate being which Hegel calls Existence and to think of coming-into-being as coming-into-existence or passing-away as passing-out-of-existence. But precisely that being from which the movement of Becoming is said to come or towards which it is said to go *is* only as the result of this process of

determination. Since Being and Nothing acquire reality only in Becoming, in Becoming, as the mere transition "from-to," neither one is
determined in opposition to the other. What we have is thought's
first truth: Becoming is not determined as coming-into-being and
passing-away on the basis of a pregiven difference of Being and Nothing, rather, this difference emerges from Becoming in thinking the
determination of Becoming as transition. Being and Nothing, respectively, "become" in it. Coming-into-being and passing-away are thus
the self-determining truth of Becoming. They balance each other out,
as it were, insofar as there is in them no other determination than the
directionality implied in "from-to," which in turn is determined only
by the difference in direction. The equilibrium between coming-into-
being and passing-away of which Hegel speaks is only another way of
expressing the utter lack of difference constitutive of Being and Nothing. Indeed, it is correct to say that it is open to us to see in Becoming something either coming into being or something passing away.
Coming-into-being is, if viewed in reference to Existence, just as
much passing-away and vice versa—as Hölderlin in his well-known
treatise on "Becoming in Passing-Away" quite properly assumes.

If, then, we wish to be clear about the development from Becoming
to Existence, the deeper sense of Hegel's dialectical deduction, i.e.,
that beyond what is immediately and generally illuminating in it,
must be stated as follows: since the distinction between Being and
Nothing is without content, there is also no determinateness present
in the "from" and "to" constituting Becoming. All that is implied is
that there is in every case a "from-to" and that every "from-to" can
be thought of as a "from-where" or a "to-where." Thus we have here
the pure structure of transition itself. The special characteristic of
Becoming is that its content, a being which is not nothing, issues
from this structure. Thought has now gone so far as to determine itself henceforth as being which is not nothing. As Hegel expresses it,
the still unity of Existence results replacing the shifting equilibrium
of coming-into-being and passing-away.

Our retracing of Hegel's dialectical deduction here should now have
enabled us to see why the question of how movement gets into the
concept of Being cannot arise in the first place. For in fact, no movement does get into Being. Being, as well as Nothing, may not be taken
as existences already "there" outside of thought, but rather as pure
thoughts along with which nothing is to be imagined except themselves. They do not occur at all save in the movement of thought.
Whoever asks how movement starts in Being should admit that in

raising that question he has abstracted from the movement of thought within which he finds himself raising it. But instead, he leaves this reflection aside thinking it "external reflection." Certainly in Being just as in Nothing, nothing determinate is thought. What is present is empty intuiting or thinking, but that means no real intuiting or thinking. But even if nothing other than empty intuiting or thinking is present, the movement of self-determination, that is, of Becoming, is there. "One has acquired great insight when one realizes that being and not-being are abstractions without truth and that the first truth is Becoming alone" (XIII 306).

Our investigation of the beginning of the *Logic* has led us to the point where we can see that Hegel's claim of immanent necessity for the dialectical development of his thought is not touched by the usual objections to the fact that the *Logic* begins with Being and Nothing. If one keeps the purpose which Hegel assigned to the *Logic* in mind, his claim that its dialectic is scientific proves to be thoroughly consistent. It is another question, however, whether that purpose, which he proposes for his *Logic* as transcendental logic, is justified convincingly when even he himself relies on the natural logic which he finds in the "logical instinct" of language. The expression, "instinct," which Hegel uses here, apparently means the unconscious, but unerring tendency towards a goal, a tendency such as that which seems to make animal behavior virtually compulsive. For that is the nature of instinct: unconsciously and, precisely for that reason, unerringly, it does everything which, if one were aware of it, one would like to have done in order to reach a goal. When Hegel speaks of the logical instinct of language he is thus pointing out the direction and object of thought—its tendency towards "the logical." In the first place, it should be noted that that term has quite a comprehensive meaning. And to be sure, there is reflected in language—not only in its grammatical, syntactical forms, but also in its nouns—that tendency of reason to objectify which was the essential characteristic of the Greek *logos*. What is thought and what is said is so constituted that one can point to it, as it were, even if one takes no position with regard to the truth of what is said and so that, on the contrary, even where the question of its truth is left unasked, the tendency of reason to objectify is actualized and precisely that gives thinking and speaking its special character of being universally objectifying. Thus Aristotle singled out the *logos apophantikos* from all other modes of speech because his sole concern was with making things plain (*dēloun*). In so doing he established propositional logic, the logic which prevailed completely until only very recently when it was shown to have its limits by Hans Lipps's *Hermeneutic Logic* and Austin's *How to Do Things with Words*,[3] to take two examples. Hegel, however, radicalizes the Aristotelian tradition not only by utilizing dialectic, but also, and indeed above all, by giving conceptual form in his *Logic* to the structure of dialectic itself. To be sure, the actual "logical" determinations constitutive of the relationships of things thought to each other, e.g., identity, difference, relation, proportion, etc., or those determinations which Plato compared to the vowels (*Sophist* 253), are always operative only when wrapped in language as it were. Thus in grammar there is a reflection of these logical structures. But Hegel's talk of the "logical instinct" of language obviously implies more than that. It means that language leads us to logic because in logic the categories naturally at work in language are focused on as such. For Hegel, language thus reaches its perfection in the idea of logic since in the latter thinking goes through all of the determinations of thought occurring within itself and operating in the natural logic of language, and relates these to each other in thinking the Concept as such.

But the question arises whether language is in fact only an instinctive logic waiting to be penetrated by thought and conceptualized. Hegel notes the correspondence between logic and grammar and compares—without heed to the differences between languages and their grammatical bases—the life which a "dead" grammar assumes in the actual use of a language to the life which logic assumes when one gives content to its dead form through use of it in positive sciences. But as much as logic and grammar might correspond to each other in that both are what they are in concrete use, the natural logic lying in the grammar of every language is by no means exhausted in the function of being a prefiguration of philosophic logic. Of course, logic in its traditional form is a purely formal science, and thus in any specific use made of it in the sciences or elsewhere, it is one and the same; the life which it assumes for the knower in such use is its proper life. On the other hand, the idea of logic which Hegel develops within the tradition of Kant's transcendental analytic, is not formal in this sense. That, however. seems to me to have a consequence which Hegel would not desire. Specifically, its use in the

3. Hans Lipps, *Untersuchungen zu einer Hermeneutischen Logik,* Frankfurt, 1953, and Austin, *How to Do Things with Words.* (TRANS.)

sciences is by no means the only concretion of this logic. (Indeed the one-sidedness of neo-Kantianism lay in the fact that it turned the given fact of science into a monopoly.) On the contrary, in the "variety of human language structures"[4] there lies a range of very different anticipations of what is logical, which are articulated in the most diverse schemata of linguistic access to the world. And the "logical instinct," which most assuredly does lie in language as such, can for that reason never be comprehensive enough to include all of what is prefigured in this vast number of languages. Thus it could never really be elevated to its "concept" by being transformed into logic.

If one keeps in mind the relationship which, as noted above, obtains between the operative use of concepts on the one hand and their express thematization on the other, and if one realizes that there is no possibility of getting around that relationship, one cannot remain indifferent to the problem which is implied here. What holds for the construction of the *Logic*—namely that it must already presuppose and use the categories of reflection which it then claims to deduce dialectically—holds for every relationship between word and concept. With words too, there is no beginning ex nihilo. Nor is it the case that a concept could be determined as a concept without the usage of the word with all of its many meanings playing a role. Thus it does not appear coincidental to me that Hegel's acute analysis and dialectical deduction of categories is always most convincing where he appends a historic derivation of the word. Concepts are only what they are in their functioning and this functioning always rests on the natural logic of language. Strictly speaking, it is not a matter of our making use of words when we speak. Though we "use" words, it is not in the sense that we put a given tool to use as we please. Words themselves prescribe the only ways in which we can put them to use. One refers to that as proper "usage"—something which does not depend on us, but rather we on it, since we are not allowed to violate it.

Now Hegel, assuredly, is conscious of this when he speaks of the "natural logic." The concept too is not a tool of our thinking, rather our thinking obeys it and finds the prefiguration of it in the natural logic of language. Precisely for this reason the task of the *Logic*—to thematize what "one thinks," in respect to itself, in "pure thinking"—confronts us with an insoluble problem. Hegel discovers this

4. "Verschiedenheit des Menschlichen Sprachbaus" (Wilhelm von Humboldt). (TRANS.)

problem and takes it to be that of the inherent disquietude of the
dialectical process. Nevertheless, that process is supposed to be super-
seded in absolute knowing as thinking of the totality. The question
arises, however, whether this "supposed to be" does not suffer from
the "immorality" of a "supposed to be" which is never able to overcome its untruth.[5]

Truly, our human nature is so much determined by finitude that
the phenomenon of language and the thinking wherein we seek to get
hold of it must always be viewed as governed by the law of human
finitude. Seen in this way, language is not a transitional form of thinking reason which is perfected when thought becomes completely
transparent to itself. It is not a self-effacing and temporary medium
of thought or merely its "casing." And its function is not at all limited
to merely making plain what is being thought of beforehand. On the
contrary, a thought first attains determinate existence in being formulated in words. Thus, it turns out that the movement of language
goes in two directions: it aims towards the objectivity of the thought,
but it also returns from it in the reabsorption of all objectification
into the sustaining[6] power and shelter of the word. When Hegel undertook to uncover "the logical" as that "innermost" in language and to
present it in its entire dialectical self-differentiation, he was correct in
seeing this undertaking as the attempt to reconstruct in thought the
thoughts of God before the creation—a reality prior to reality. But
even that reality or "Being" standing at the beginning of this con-
templative repetition in our thought, the content of which is ultimately to be fully objectified in the concept, always presupposes language in which thinking has its own abode. The *Phenomenology of
Spirit*, where Hegel methodically leads up to the beginning of pure
thought, does not furnish us with this presupposition, but rather it,
too, constantly presupposes the functioning of language which sustains

5. The reference here is to Hegel's critique of Fichte's attempt to build idealism on an ethical foundation. Cf. Hegel's critique of *Sollen* (L I 111), where he
treats *Sollen* as a form of the "bad infinity." (TRANS.)

6. *Bergend.* A key word—tied to *Unverborgenheit*—in Heidegger's thought.
Cf., for example, "Der Ursprung des Kunstwerkes," *Holzwege,* Frankfurt,
1963, pp. 7 ff. Implied is the double sense of concealing, on the one hand, of
sheltering and sustaining, on the other. Things which are in "truth" (*alētheia*)
are *unverborgen*, which is to say disconcealed, and at the same time grounded
in their sheltering source (*geborgen*). Gadamer sees language as just such a
source of what is, hence his phrase, "die bergende Gewalt des Wortes."
(TRANS.)

and accompanies it. Thus it itself remains tied to the idea of total objectification of self and fulfills itself in absolute knowing. Its insurmountable limitation becomes manifest in our experience of language. What makes it possible for language to speak is not "Being" as the abstract immediacy of the self-determining concept. Rather, it is much better described in terms of the being which Heidegger refers to as a "clearing." A clearing, however, implies both something disclosed and something still enclosed.

A kind of thinking, able to conceive of the functioning of language as revealing and objectifying but at the same time as holding back or concealing as well, can find in Hegel's attempt at logic only one side of the truth—that of the perfected determination of the concept. Still to have established only this one-sidedness is not sufficient. Were it taken to be, then an essential concern common to both Heidegger and Hegel would have been overlooked. Specifically, Hegel's logic indirectly points beyond itself, since Hegel's turn of speech, "the logical," of which he is so fond, indicates that the essential impossibility of completing the concept is acknowledged by him. "The logical" is not the quintessence or totality of all determinations of thought but the dimension which underlies all posited determinations of thought, just as a geometric continuum underlies all posited points. Hegel calls it the "speculative" dimension and speaks of the "speculative statement" which, as opposed to all statement sentences referring a predicate to a subject, demands a retreat of thought into itself. The speculative statement maintains the mean between the extremes of tautology on the one hand and self-cancelation in the infinite determination of its meaning on the other. Here lies Hegel's great relevance for today: the speculative statement is not so much a statement as it is language. It calls for more than objectification in dialectical explication. While it does call for such explication, at the same time the speculative statement brings dialectical movement to a standstill. Through it thought is made to see itself in relationship to itself. In the language form (not of a judgment as a statement, but in the judgment as it is *spoken* in a verdict, for example, or in the curse) the event of its being said is felt, and not merely what is said.[7]

7. At this point Gadamer comes very close to developing a theory of what Austin refers to as illocutionary meaning. Cf. Austin, *How to Do Things with Words,* chapter 8, pp. 94 ff. Still his basic concern remains quite different from Austin's. For Gadamer the issue is not "how to do things with words," but rather how words and language constitute the significance of the world in

Mutatis mutandis, in the speculative statement the event of thinking
is present. The speculative statement which challenges and stirs
thought in this way thus unmistakably "consists in itself" as do,
more generally, words of poetry and the being of the artwork. In the
"consisting in itself" of poetry and artworks there is an assertion
which "stands" self-contained. And just as the speculative statement
demands dialectical "exposition," the work of art demands interpretation, even though its content may never be exhausted in any particular interpretation. My point is that the speculative statement is not
a judgment restricted in the content of what it asserts any more than
a single word without a context or a communicative utterance torn
from its context is a self-contained unit of meaning. The words
which someone utters are tied to the continuum in which people
come to understand each other, the continuum which determines the
word to such an extent that it can even be "taken back." Similarly,
the speculative statement points to an entirety of truth, without
being this entirety or stating it. Hegel conceives of this entirety which
is not in actual existence as the reflection in itself through which the
entirety proves to be the truth of the concept. Having been compelled
by the speculative statement to follow the path of conceptual comprehension, thought unfolds "the logical" as the immanent movement of its content.

Though within this tendency towards "the logical" it is the concept
which is thought of as the completed determination of the indeterminate, and though in that concept only the one aspect of language
(its tendency towards "the logical") is completely developed, reflection's being or consisting in itself nevertheless continues to have a
disconcerting similarity to the "consisting in itself" of the word and
of the artwork which bear truth contained (*geborgen*) within themselves. Indeed, there is a hint here of that conception of "truth"
which Heidegger seeks to formulate in his thought as the "event of
being" and which opens up the space for the movement of reflection,
as well as for all knowledge, in the first place.

----

which we find ourselves underway. Gadamer's questioning here derives from
transcendental philosophy—he is asking about the "condition of the possibility" of our experience, to use Kant's phrase, but from a different ontological
perspective from that of Kantian philosophy. The "condition of the possibility" is not to be grounded in the subject, but rather the subject in it. Thus instead of asking how we do things with words, Gadamer asks, in effect, how
words do things with us. (TRANS.)

Again and again Heidegger himself bears witness to this wider inference of "the speculative" and the temptation it presents. This is revealed not only in the fascination Hegel's dialectic has for him, in the critical analyses which it prompts and in his effort to differentiate his own philosophy from it. Beyond all of this there are occasional direct references to Hegel, rich in illuminating advertences, which we ought now to include in our discussion. Most important of these is the sketch of an idea found in his *Nietzsche*,[8] vol. 2, p. 464:

> Reflection, grasped within the history of being in its being-thereness. The light shining back to *alētheia* without the latter itself being experienced as such and being grounded and coming into its proper presence ("*Wesen*"). The homelessness of the shining back of what shows itself . . . man's settlement in one of his proper places of presence. Reflection—certainty, certainty—self-consciousness.

Here Heidegger refers to reflection as a "shining back into *alētheia* without the latter itself . . . coming into its proper presence." Thus he himself relates reflection to that which he conceives of as *alētheia* and which he calls here the being of *alētheia* as it presents itself. To be sure, establishing this relationship amounts to making a distinction at the same time: the dimension of "the logical" is not the sphere of *alētheia* which is illumined by language. For language is an "element" within which we live in a very different sense than reflection is.[9] Language completely surrounds us like the voice of home which prior to our every thought of it breathes a familiarity from time out of mind. Heidegger refers to language as the "house of being," in which we dwell with such ease. To be sure, there occurs in it, indeed precisely in it, the disconcealment of what is present to the point of the objectification of the latter in a statement. But being itself, which has its abode there, is not disconcealed as such, but keeps itself concealed in the midst of all disconcealment occurring in speaking; concealed as in speaking, language itself remains essentially concealed. Thus Heidegger is not saying in any way that reflection takes the measure of this original "clearing." Rather, he speaks of reflection as the shining back of what is showing itself; while never

8. Heidegger, *Nietzsche,* Pfullingen, 1961.
9. The word "element" figures prominently in Heidegger's thought after his "Kehre." Cf. *Über den Humanismus,* Bern, 1954, p. 56. (TRANS.)

ceasing to be underway within the "clearing," reflection seeks to get this shining back in view before itself. In this respect reflection, the movement of logic, is homeless: it can stay nowhere. That which shows itself, i.e., that which is encountered as the object of thought and of the process of determination, has the "object's" essential mode of being encountered. That accounts for its insurmountable "transcendence" for thought, which in turn prevents us from being at home in it. The process of comprehension which aims nevertheless at eliminating this transcendence and which Hegel unfolds as the basic movement of self-recognition in the other, is for that reason continually thrown back on itself. As a result it has the character of the self-assuring process of self-consciousness. This too is a manner of appropriation and as such, it provides the "housing" which has given Western civilization its essential form—making what is another one's own means the conquest and subjugation of nature through work. Heidegger is not striking up the song of cultural criticism here. Rather, in the comment which we are explicating he speaks of what has occurred as "man's settlement in one of his proper places of presence." Because this "settlement" constitutes all that exists as "object," it is in an essential sense, he maintains, the "expropriation event (*Ent-eignung*) of what exists."[10] What exists does not belong to itself because it is entirely there in reference to us. Viewed in this way, Hegel appears as the logical consummation of a path of thought going back a long way—an end in which the subsequent philosophical phenomena of Marx and logical positivism are foreshadowed.

Nevertheless, that which escapes this perspective of thought comes to light here—that which Schelling sensed first and which Heidegger developed into the question about the being which is not the being of existents. The shining back of what shows itself—incidentally, a literal translation of "reflection"—is certainly different from the original "clearing" in which what is comes to show itself in the first place. There is indeed another familiarity, one more basic than that acquired and cultivated in appropriation, which prevails where word and language are at work.

Still, it is nothing less than the complete fathoming of an essential course of human thought when Hegel in "reflection in itself" thinks the light "shining back" which all objectification casts. In Hegel's reflection-in-itself, which unfolds as the movement of the *Logic*,

---

10. *Ent-eignung* is one of Heidegger's multiple variations on the stem, *eignen.* Cf. *Identität und Differenz,* Pfullingen, 1957, especially p. 33 (TRANS.)

there is preserved a truth which is not that of consciousness and its opposite, that is, a truth, precisely, which in no way claims to be the "appropriation" of what shows itself, but rather distinguishes such "external" reflection as that, from the reflection of thought into itself. That is what emerges in Hegel's *Logic*. If one traces the experience of consciousness in the way Hegel does in the *Phenomenology*, namely, in such a way that one learns to recognize everything alien as one's own, one sees that the lesson actually taught to consciousness is none other than the experience which thinking has with its "pure" thoughts. Still it is not only the *Phenomenology* which points beyond itself, i.e., in its case, to the *Logic*. For its part, does not the logic of the self-unfolding concept necessarily point beyond itself too, that is, point back to the "natural logic" of language? The self of the concept (in which pure thinking conceives of itself) is, in the last analysis, nothing of the sort which displays itself, but rather, like language, something at work in everything which is. The determinations of the *Logic* are not without the "casing" of language in which thought is sheathed. The medium of reflection in which the progression of the *Logic* moves is for its part, however, not sheathed in language like the conceptual determination at any given point, but rather, as an entirety, as the "logical," is in shining back, grounded in illumination of language. Indirectly, that is made evident in Heidegger's note.

Were Hegel's idea of logic to include full acknowledgment of its relationship to the natural logic, which he treats on the level of reflective consciousness, he would have to draw close again to the classical origin of his idea in Plato's dialectic and Aristotle's conquest of sophism through logic. As it stands, his logic remains a grand realization of the goal of thinking "the logical" as the foundation of all objectification. Thus, Hegel brought to its completion the development of traditional logic into a transcendental "logic of objectivity"—a development which began with Fichte's "Doctrine of Science." But the language-ness of all thought continues to demand that thought, moving in the opposite direction, convert the concept back into the valid word. The more radically objectifying thought reflects upon itself and unfolds the experience of dialectic, the more clearly it points to what it is not. Dialectic must retrieve itself in hermeneutics.

5

Hegel and Heidegger

Heidegger is probably not the first to have formulated the theory that Hegel represents the consummation of Western metaphysics. It is all too clearly written in the language of historical facts that the two thousand year tradition which shaped Western philosophy came to an end in Hegel's system and in its sudden collapse in the middle of the nineteenth century. Not the least evidence of this is the fact that philosophy since then has been a purely academic concern, or put another way, that only authors outside of academia such as Schopenhauer and Kierkegaard, Marx and Nietzsche along with the great novelists of the nineteenth and twentieth centuries have succeeded in reaching the consciousness of the period and in satisfying its need for a philosophical vision of the world. But when Heidegger speaks of the consummation of Western metaphysics which Hegel achieves, he is not only speaking of an historical fact. He is at the same time specifying a task which lies before us, that of "overcoming metaphysics," as he calls it. In this way of putting the matter "metaphysics" does not only refer to the ultimate form of metaphysics which comes into being and then collapses with Hegel's system of absolute idealism. A reference is also made thereby to the inception of metaphysics in the thought of Plato and Aristotle and even to metaphysics as it endures in its basic form in versions of it which reach into modern times and which, it may even be said, provide the foundation of modern science. For precisely that reason "overcoming" metaphysics can be no mere putting it behind us, no mere divorcing of ourselves from the older tradition of metaphysical thought. On the contrary, "overcoming" (*Überwinden*) implies, as Heidegger's inimitable way with language and thinking brings out, "getting over," in the sense of "coming to grips with" (*Verwinden*). That which we "get over" or "come to grips with" is not simply past and forgotten. Getting over a loss, for example, consists not merely in our gradually forgetting it and "taking it." Or better, let us say that we do in fact "take it," but in the sense that the pain is dealt with rather than that it gradually lets up. And far from being gone without a trace, the pain

in our conscious achievement of enduring it, lastingly and irrevocably
determines our own being. We stay with it, as it were, even when we
have gotten over it. That is particularly appropriate for Hegel, for one
must "stay with" him in a special way.

The assertion that Hegel represents the consummation of metaphysics shares a certain ambiguity which, as a matter of fact, characterizes the special role which Hegel plays in the history of Western
thought. Is his thought the end? Is it a completion or fulfillment?
Is this completion or end the fulfillment of Christian thought in the
concept of philosophy, or is it the end and dissolution of everything
Christian in the thought of the modern period? The claim which
Hegel's philosophy makes contains in it an equivocation which in
turn is responsible for the fact that this man assumes the historical
role he does. Does a philosophy of history in which freedom as the
essence of man reaches the level of self-consciousness, hold this self-
consciousness of freedom to be the end of history? Or does history
at the end only now assume its proper form insofar as only in the
consciousness of the freedom of all, i.e., in this Christian or revolutionary consciousness, history first becomes the battle for freedom?
Hegel characterizes the philosophy of absolute knowledge as the
standpoint of philosophy which, he says, thinking has now reached as
the result of the grand historical past of thought. Does such absolute
knowledge imply that finally all errors lie behind us? Or is that philosophy of absolute knowledge a first encounter with the entirety of
our history, one such that afterwards historical consciousness will
never again let us out of its grip? When Hegel, from the viewpoint of
the philosophy of the absolute concept, speaks of art as a thing of the
past, even this astounding and provocative assertion is highly ambiguous. Is he saying that art no longer has a purpose, no longer states
anything? Or did he mean that art is a thing of the past in respect to
the standpoint of absolute concept, because it was always and will
always be preliminary to conceptual thinking? In that case the "past-
ness" of art would only be the "speculative" way of expressing the
contemporaneousness which distinguishes it. On this view, it would
not be subject to the laws of progress governing speculative thought
as the latter first comes to itself in the development of philosophy.
Thus Heidegger's ambiguous formulation, "the consummation of
metaphysics," leads us finally to an ambiguity common to Hegel and
Heidegger. Concisely stated, the issue here is whether or not the comprehensive mediation of every conceivable path of thought, which
Hegel undertook, might not of necessity give the lie to every attempt

to break out of the circle of reflection in which thought thinks itself. In the end, is even the position which Heidegger tries to establish in opposition to Hegel trapped within the sphere of the inner infinity of reflection?

Indeed, the latent presence which characterized Hegel's thought as it endured through the period when it appeared forgotten—a latent presence which filled Germany in the second half of the nineteenth century—shows us that the actuality of his thought remained insurmountable. That actuality is not only confirmed by the open and explicit return to his thought and reconsideration of it as that occurred in Italy, Holland, and England and then subsequently, in the twentieth century, as it was cultivated in Germany in the form of academic neo-Hegelianism. Nor, moreover, does the transformation of philosophy into politics or into neo-Marxian ideology-critique suffice to confirm it entirely. To be sure, in the period after Hegel philosophy assumed new forms, but it was always as critiques of metaphysics that positivism, epistemology, philosophy of science, phenomenology, or language analysis felt surest of themselves. In metaphysics, the field he might call his very own, Hegel had no followers. As those fading neo-Kantians affecting an Hegelian mode of thought were quick to recognize, it remained for Heidegger to transform the final and most powerful form of neo-Kantian thought, i.e., Husserl's phenomenology, into philosophy. Or, if one wishes to apply another standard, it is Heidegger who made it appear that thought must finally awaken from Husserl's dream of philosophy as a strict science. It is in this respect that Heidegger's thought draws close to Hegel's philosophy. Of course half a century—it has been that long that Heidegger's thought has been having its effect on us—does not suffice to guarantee him a permanent rank in world history. Still there is a certain negative documentation that when one places Heidegger's philosophical work alongside of Hegel's in the history of great, classical thinkers one is not overestimating him. Just as Hegel's thought completely dominated Germany for a period of time and from that base ultimately dominated Europe, only then to collapse completely, Heidegger for a long period was the dominant thinker for his contemporaries on the German scene. And correspondingly, the rejection of him today is total. We are still waiting for a Karl Marx who would resist treating Heidegger as Marx, though opposing him, resisted treating the great thinker, Hegel—as a "dead dog."

The question which must be asked here is one to be taken quite

seriously: is Heidegger's thinking to be placed within the borders of
Hegel's empire of thought as is, for instance, the thought of all the
"young Hegelians" or neo-Kantian critics of Hegel from Feuerbach
and Kierkegaard to Husserl and Jaspers? Or do all the correspon-
dences to Hegel which Heidegger's thought indisputably displays
prove precisely the opposite—namely that his questioning is radical
and comprehensive enough to have left out nothing which Hegel asks
and at the same time to have asked still more deeply than Hegel did
and thus to have gotten behind him? If the latter should be the case,
incidentally, it would have the consequence of altering the picture we
have of Hegel's place in the history of the movement of Idealism as a
whole. For one thing, Fichte would be seen to occupy a more independent position. For another, Schelling's presentiments would be
borne out and unseen truths would emerge from the desperate reck-
lessness of Nietzsche's thought.

It would then no longer be remarkable at all that in Heidegger's
thought a most astonishing event in the history of world literature,
the discovery in the twentieth century of one of the greatest German
poets, Friederich Hölderlin, took on epoch making proportions.
Hölderlin, who suffered misfortune both as a poet and as a man, had
remained, as we know, a close friend of Hegel's since the days of
their youth, and even though the Romantic school of German poets
and, thereafter, Nietzsche and Dilthey displayed a certain liking and
admiration for him, it is only in our century that he permanently assumed his rightful place alongside of the greatest German poets. The
fact that he also became the virtual key to Heidegger's thought confirms in quite an unexpected way that Hölderlin is contemporaneous
with this century, however curious it might be that his contemporaneousness was delayed. And it confirms furthermore, that a juxtaposition of Heidegger's thought and Hegel's philosophy is neither
contrived nor arbitrary.

It is striking enough how persistently Heidegger's thought circles
around Hegel and how he continues even to this day to seek new
ways of demarcating his own thought from Hegel's. Of course that
is also a reflection of the vitality of Hegel's dialectic, a method which
continues to reassert itself in opposition to Husserl's and Heidegger's
phenomenological procedure. Indeed, Hegel's dialectical method
suppressed the latter to such an extent that the carefully cultivated
craftsmanship of phenomenology is now forgotten and the art of it
no longer practiced. There is more at stake here than the question
which many have put to the later Heidegger, specifically, how his

convincing critique of idealism at the level of consciousness, which, when it appeared in *Being and Time,* ushered in a new era in philosophy, could be upheld in opposition to Hegel's philosophy of mind (*Geist*). That it could appears all the more uncertain since Heidegger himself, after the "turning," abandoned his transcendental conception of self, on the one hand, and *Dasein*'s understanding of being as the point of departure for posing the question about being, on the other. Does he not draw close to Hegel in this? For it is Hegel who explicitly carried the dialectic mind or spirit beyond the forms of subjective spirit, beyond consciousness and self-consciousness. Furthermore, in the view of all those who seek to defend themselves against the claims of Heidegger's thought, there is one point in particular where Heidegger seems to converge again and again with Hegel's speculative idealism. That is in his inclusion of history in the framework of philosophy's questioning.

That he does include it is certainly neither a coincidence nor without reason. It seems to be a fundamental trait of philosophical consciousness in the nineteenth century that it is no longer conceivable apart from historical consciousness. Plainly, behind this fact lies the break with the traditional European world of Christian states which was brought about by the French Revolution. The Revolution's radical attempt to make the Enlightenment's faith in reason the basis of religion, state, and society had the counter effect of bringing historical relativity and the power of history into general awareness; for history is that which decisively rebutted the presumptuous excesses of the Revolution's "new beginning." The historical consciousness emerging at this point required new proof of the legitimacy of philosophy's claim to be knowledge. Every philosophical attempt to add something new to the Greco-Christian tradition of thought now had to give a historical justification of itself, and an attempt where such a justification was not forthcoming or was inadequate would of necessity lack the power to reach and convince the general consciousness. In particular, that became painfully clear to Wilhelm Dilthey, the thinker of historicism.

Seen in this light, the radical and comprehensive fashion in which Hegel achieved the historical self-justification of his philosophy appears overwhelmingly superior to all later attempts. He united nature and history under the rule of this all-inclusive concept of the *logos,* which in times before the Greeks had exalted in laying the foundation for their *prima philosophia.* In viewing the world as divinely created, the earlier theodicy of the age of the Enlightenment had pointed to the mathematical rationality of events in nature. Hegel now extends this claim of divine rationality to history. Just as the Greeks had taught that *logos* or *nous* was the essence and ground of the universe in spite of the disorder and irrationality of the sublunar world, Hegel now teaches us that reason can be discovered in history in spite of the frightful contradictoriness which the chaos of human fate and history displays. Thus that which had previously been left to faith and trust in providence because of its impenetrability for human knowing and insight, he now brings within the realm of thought.

Dialectic was the magic charm enabling Hegel to uncover a necessity in the erratic drifting of human history, a necessity as convincing and rational as that which for ages past, and in the modern era of natural science as well, had been evident in the lawfulness and order of nature. As his point of departure here Hegel took the Ancients' conception of dialectic as essentially being the heightening of contradictions. The Ancients, however, held that the working out of dialectical contradictions was only a study which prepared one for actual knowing. Hegel, on the other hand, converts this propaedeutic or negative purpose of dialectic into a positive one. For Hegel the point of dialectic is that precisely by pushing a position to the point of self-contradiction it makes possible the transition to a higher truth which unites the sides of that contradiction: the power of spirit lies in synthesis as the mediation of all contradictions.

What Hegel is proposing here is expressed clearly in the changed meaning which *Aufhebung* acquires in his work. Originally, the word had had a negative sense. Specifically, in the demonstration that something is contradictory its validity is *aufgehoben*, which is to say, canceled or negated. For Hegel, however, the meaning shifts and comes to imply preservation of all the elements of truth, which assert themselves within the contradictions, and even an elevation of these elements to a truth encompassing and uniting everything true. In this way dialectic becomes the advocate of the "concrete" or mediated truth over against the one-sided abstractions of the understanding. Reason's universal power of synthesis is not only able to mediate the oppositions in thought, but also to sublimate the oppositions in the real world. It demonstrates exactly this in history insofar as the most alien, inscrutable, and inimical forces of history are surmounted by reason's power of reconciliation. Reason is reconciliation with ruination.

Hegel's dialectic of history grows out of the problem to which the

social consciousness of the waning eighteenth century addressed itself and which especially engaged its young academics, stirred as they
were by the impact of the French Revolution. At the time when the
effects of the emancipation of the Third Estate reached the German
Reich, the latter found itself in most unhappy circumstances, for it
had been clear for some time that under the present conditions its
constitution was archaic. Thus as early as the time of Hegel's study
in Tübingen the young generation had raised the cry for a new "identification with the universal" in all matters—in Christianity as well as
in the socio-political reality.

The model which the young Hegel made basic to his exposition of
this "identification with the universal" was an example of extreme
alienation: the split between the criminal and the law of the society.
The inimical other which the law, in requiring that he be punished,
represents to the criminal being prosecuted, appears to Hegel to be
the paradigm for all divisions pervading that declining era, which was
so much in need of rejuvenation. Now from Hegel's point of view the
essence of punishment is to be thought of as restoration of the just
order of law. He recognizes that even for the one to whom it is
applied, the proper nature of punishment and the legal significance
of it, does not consist in the hostility which the penal authority displays towards the criminal. On the contrary, the purpose of the punishment is realized, and justice brought about only when the criminal
accepts his punishment. That acceptance returns the criminal to life
in the community of law. In this way punishment converts from the
hostile force which it had represented into that which brings about
reunification. And that, precisely, is the "reconciliation with ruination"—a splendid formulation in which Hegel expresses the universal
essence of this event.

To be sure, Hegel's line of thought concerning punishment develops
in response to a particular theological problem, specifically the question of how forgiveness of sins is to be reconciled with the righteous-
ness of God. Thus, it specifically focuses upon the inner meaning of
the relationship between faith and grace. Still, the phenomenon illustrated here, that of a conversion or turnabout from hostility to friend-
liness, has universal significance. Friederich Schiller was the first to
recognize the problem to which Hegel assigns a central role, the problem of the alienation of self and the overcoming of it (cf. Schiller's
letters on aesthetics).[1] Later Marx was to make that problem central

1. F. Schiller, *Über die Ästhetische Erziehung des Menschen, Werke,* ed.
Guntter und Witkowski, pt. 17, 1910.

to his analysis of the practical realm. For his part Hegel sees in reason, which unites all contradictions, the universal structure of reality. The essence of spirit lies in its capacity to transform what stands opposed to it into its own, or, as Hegel prefers to express it, to attain knowledge of itself in what is another and in this way, to transcend alienation. Underlying the power of spirit is the structure of dialectic, which, as the universal constitutive form of reality, also governs human history. It is this structure which Hegel systematically explicates in his *Logic*.

The architecture of Hegel's *Logic*, with the three levels of Being, Essence, and Concept providing the formal, conceptual structure for spirit's return to itself, substantiates in a convincing way what Heidegger even in his earlier years had said about Hegel—that he is the most radical of the Greeks. It is not only in the basic divisions of the *Logic* where one sees the shimmer of rock strata of Greek origin shining through, for example, a Platonic, Aristotelian layer in the "Logic of Essence" and a pre-Socratic, Pythagorean one in the "Logic of Being." When the analysis reaches the specific concepts which are used, it is found that the principle of structuring these which governs the whole work also reveals the heritage of Eleatic, Platonic dialectic. The motor principle in the self-movement of each concept which is thought, proves to be its express self-contradictoriness. And the goal of this movement reached at the endpoint of spirit's way, the total transparency of the Idea to itself, represents, as it were, the triumph of reason over any and all resistance of objective reality. Thus here too Heidegger's characterization has a radical ambiguity about it: when Hegel sees reason as effective and victorious, not only in nature, but in the realm of human history as well, that constitutes a radicalization of Greek metaphysical thought about the world. But this radical extension of the *logos* can, from Heidegger's point of view, also be seen as an expression of the obliviousness to being (*Seinsvergessenheit*) towards which the modern emphasis on self-knowledge and on will that wills itself has been pointed since its inception in Greek thought.

In this light Heidegger's historical self-consciousness appears as the most extreme counterthrust possible against the project of absolute knowledge and the complete attainment of free self-consciousness—the project which Hegel makes basic to his philosophy. But precisely this fact prompts our questioning here. As is well known, Heidegger thinks that the unifying trait in the history of the metaphysical philosophy, which shapes the thought of the West in its development

from Plato to Hegel, is its mounting obliviousness to being. In that
the being of existents becomes the object of metaphysical questioning, being itself cannot be thought of in any way except that which
begins with the existent reality which forms the object of our knowing and our assertions. If we are to remain true to what Heidegger intends, the step which he demands we take behind the beginning of
metaphysical thought cannot itself be thought of as metaphysics.
Getting behind Plato and Aristotle as Hegel's *Logic* does in its first
part, "The Logic of Being," ought still to be interpreted as a kind of
preliminary metaphysics. In contrast, Nietzsche, in his embittered
polemic against Platonism and Christianity and in his discovery of
philosophy in the "Greek age of tragedy," conjures up a presentiment
of a different foreworld of thought. In laying the groundwork anew
for the question about being, Heidegger is seeking to work out the
conceptual means of making this presentiment concrete.

Heidegger, as is well known, took the anti-Greek theme in the tradition of Christian piety as his guide here. And indeed there is such
an anti-Greek motif reaching back from Luther's resolve to demand
of Christian men that they renounce Aristotle, to Gabriel Biel and
Meister Eckhart and ultimately to Augustine's profound philosophic
variations on the theme of the mystery of the Trinity. This anti-
Greek motif points to the Word of God and the act of hearing it,
which are uppermost in the Old Testament's relating of the encounter
with God. The Greek principle of *logos* and *eidos,* the articulation
and retention of the visible contours of things, appears, if viewed
from this perspective, as a falsification which does violence to the
mystery of faith. When Heidegger stirs up the question of being
again, all that is very much in evidence, and in fact, we have here the
explanation for his famous reference to the "superficiality of the
Greeks." But should it be coincidence that only now, when metaphysics has come to an end and we find ourselves entering the era of
an ascendant positivism and nihilism—that only now it becomes clear
to thought that in the half-light of the early pre-Socratics other layers
can be seen shining through the outer shell of the *logos?* The words
of Anaximander, which seemed to Schopenhauer to be a Greek version of Indian pessimism and which, in any event, he took to be an
anticipation of his own thought, begin now to sound like an anticipation of that temporal character of being which Heidegger for-
mulates as the "while." Is that coincidence? It seems difficult to me
to avoid the thought which forces itself upon us regarding Heidegger's
historical justification of himself and his return to the question of

being, specifically, that such a return is not itself a beginning, but rather, that it is made possible by an end. Can one overlook the fact that the rise of European nihilism, that positivism's crowing about the end of the "true world," which, it is said, is at long last recognized as "myth"—that all this mediates the step Heidegger takes when he directs his questioning back of metaphysics? And can this "step back" be a leap at all in the sense of a vaulting out of the medium and context of metaphysical thought? Does not history always present a continuity? Coming to be in passing away?

Of course Heidegger never speaks of an historical necessity anything like the one which Hegel claims as the basis of his construing of world history as reason in history. For Heidegger history is not a past which has been suffered through to a point where the present itself is encountered in the totality of what it has been. In his later works Heidegger quite intentionally avoids the expressions, history (*Geschichte*) and historicity (*Geschichtlichkeit*), which since Hegel have dominated reflection upon the "end of metaphysics" and which we associate with the problem of historical relativism. Instead, he speaks of "fate" (*Geschick*) and "our being fated" (*Geschicklichkeit*) as if to underscore the fact that here it is not a matter of possibilities of human existence which we ourselves seize upon—not a matter of historical consciousness and self-consciousness. Rather it is a matter of what is alloted to man and by which he is so very much determined that all self-determination and self-consciousness remains subordinate. Heidegger does not claim that in his philosophical thinking about history he grasps the necessity in the course which history takes. Nevertheless in conceiving of metaphysical thought as a history unified by the forgetfulness of being which pervades it and in seeing a radicalization of this forgetfulness behind the age of technology, he is attributing a kind of inner consequentiality to history. To go even further, if metaphysics is understood as forgetfulness of being or obliviousness to it and the history of metaphysics up to the point of its dissolution, as growing forgetfulness of being, then of necessity, it is the lot of the thinking which thinks this, that what has been forgotten comes to mind again. And, in fact, it is made evident by certain of Heidegger's phrases, e.g., "presumably, all of a sudden" (*jäh vermutlich*), that there is even a connection between increasing forgetfulness of being and the expectation of this coming or epiphany of being—a connection quite similar to that of a dialectical reversal.

In the exposure to the indeterminacy of the future which arrests all human self-projection, Heidegger finds traces of a kind of historical self-justification: the radical deepening of forgetfulness of being in the age of technology justifies the eschatological expectation in thought of a turnabout which will make visible that which actually is, behind all that produces and reproduces.

One must allow that such an historical self-consciousness as this is no less all-inclusive than Hegel's philosophy of the Absolute.

At the same time this raises a new question. Is the principle of Hegel's dialectic really to be tied to its extreme implication, i.e., that entailed by the transparency of the idea to itself or spirit's self-consciousness, respectively? To be sure, in making indeterminate, immediate Being the point of departure for the *Logic*, Hegel establishes the meaning of Being as "absolute determinacy." But is it not constitutive of the dialectical self-referentiality of philosophical thought that the truth is not a result which is dissociable from the process which led to it, but rather that it is the whole of that process, the way to the result, and nothing else? There is, of course, a temptation to try to avoid the self-apotheosis of thought implied in Hegel's idea of truth by denying it outright and juxtaposing to it, as Heidegger does, the temporality and finitude of human existence, or even by contradicting it as Adorno does, when he asserts that the whole is not true but false. Still it can be asked whether this does justice to Hegel. The ambiguities, which Hegel's doctrines so abundantly display and which our examples at the beginning served to illustrate, are of positive significance in the final analysis: they prevent us from thinking of the concept of the whole and ultimately, therefore, of the concept of Being, in terms of total determinacy.

On the contrary, the all-encompassing synthesis which Hegel's speculative idealism claims to accomplish contains an unresolved tension—one which is reflected in the way in which the meaning of the word "dialectic" shifts in Hegel. Specifically, "dialectical" may be said on the one hand to characterize the viewpoint of reason, which is able to perceive both the unity of the whole and the whole of the unity in all oppositions and contradictions. But, on the other hand, dialectic, corresponding to the meaning of the word in antiquity, is also thought of as the heightening of all contradictions to a "fixed" point of irresolvable contradictoriness, or, put another way, as the working out of the contradictions that plunge thought into an abyss of meaningless talk, even if from the perspective of reason the contradictions coexist in tension filled unity. Now and then, in order to stress this difference, Hegel refers to the point of view of reason as "speculative"

meaning by that that it is "positive-reasonable." In so doing he is taking dialectic to refer to the process character of philosophical demonstration, i.e., to the process of making explicit the contradictions
which are implied and overcome in what is "positive-reasonable."
Plainly, there is an ambivalence at the root of this. On the one hand,
there is Hegel's reliance upon the ideal method of objectification in
thought, a method which was finally raised to the level of self-
consciousness in Descartes and which assumes its ultimate form in
Hegel's logical panmethodism. On the other hand, though, there is
the concrete experience of reason which precedes this ideal method
of philosophical demonstration and which makes clear in the first
place the possibility of the latter and what its purpose is. We have
come across this experience already in the power of "reconciliation
with ruination." Further evidence of its importance is given in the
way in which Hegel works out his *Logic*. For the totality of the determinations of thought, the dialectical entirety of the categories, presupposes the dimension of thought itself, which Hegel designates
with the monotheistic singular, "the logical." When Heidegger says
that a thinker only thinks of the end, that can certainly be applied to
Hegel. For Hegel sees the unity of the speculative and reasonable in
everything, and, as is well known, he said of Heraclitus's cryptic utterances, which are manifold variations on this principle of speculative
unity, that there was not a single one which he had failed to incorporate in his *Logic*. The masterful way in which Hegel, in working out
the historical tradition of philosophy, uncovers everywhere the same
thing again and again, stands in plain opposition to and clearly prevails over the despotic superciliousness which he displays when he
claims to have pointed out limitations in earlier thinking and demonstrated the "necessity" in the history of philosophy, the odyssey of
thought. For that reason it often appears that one need only stretch
Hegel's interpretation of the history of philosophy slightly to make
the "positive-reasonable" content in earlier thinking evident beyond
a doubt.

But in Heidegger's case, things are not so very different. To be sure,
the history of metaphysics is articulated in his thought as "being's
fate for us" (*Seinsgeschick*), which is seen as determining both the
present and the future. And according to its inner necessity this history, the history of obliviousness to being, moves towards its most
radical consequence. But Heidegger also sees the continuing influence and power of the origin of thought. It continues to prevail even
in us; it is there in Aristotle's *physis*, in the enigma of the *analogia*

entis, in Leibniz's "thirst for existence," in Schelling's "ground in God" and thus, ultimately, in Hegel's unity of the speculative and reasonable.

There is indirect evidence of the distance Hegel was able to maintain from his own method and thus also, of the proximity of Heidegger to Hegel in spite of the former's criticism of the latter for being too "Greek." That is in the relationship both have to the speculative spirit of the German language. Over the period of a century and a half we have, after all, grown accustomed to the way Hegel uses the German language in developing his concepts. Every step of the way the philosophically trained and historically oriented reader encounters the contagious power of his language in the decades of thinking where Hegel continued to prevail. The real presence which Hegel has in the language of his contemporaries does not consist in a few rickety concepts such as thesis, antithesis, and synthesis or subjective, objective, and absolute spirit. Nor, moreover, does it consist in the numerous schematic applications of these concepts which were made in the most diverse fields of research in the first half of the nineteenth century. On the contrary, it is the real power of the German language and not the schematic precision of such artificially formulated concepts as these, which breathes life into Hegel's philosophy. There is good reason for the fact that translations of him into the major cultural languages first appeared in this century—translations which without recourse to the original German text are only half-successful in communicating Hegel's train of thought. The linguistic potentialities of these other languages do not permit a direct duplication of the multiple meanings contained in such concepts as *Sein, Dasein, Wesen, Wirklichkeit, Begriff,* and *Bestimmung.* Thinking in the possible translations of these thus inevitably leads one astray into the conceptual horizons of the Scholastic metaphysics and the more modern development of their concepts. The speculative power lying in the connotations of the German words and in the range of meaning extending from them in so many directions is completely unable to penetrate the cloak of the foreign language.

Take, for instance, a sentence like that with which the second volume of the *Logic* begins (one which Heidegger as an old man discussed with his no longer very young students on the occasion of Freiburg University's Fifth Centennial Celebration)—"Die Wahrheit des Seins ist das Wesen."[2] One can take such a sentence to refer to the

2. Roughly, "the truth of being is essence," but Gadamer's point turns on

return into itself of immediate Being and to the transition from Being to the metaphysics of Essence, and that would even be in accord with Hegel's intention. The philosophy of Plato and Aristotle, which is based on the *logos,* emerges out of the inconclusiveness of Parmenides' "being" and thus the transition is made into the sphere of reflection where the key concepts are essence and form, substance, and existence. And Hegel's "history" of ancient philosophy here does in fact represent a kind of commentary on the transition from pre-Socratic to Platonic and Aristotelian thought. Nevertheless, not one of the concepts in this statement, neither *Wahrheit, Sein,* nor *Wesen,* is restricted to the conceptual horizons of metaphysics, which, in Latin concepts and the subsequent elaboration and differentiation of them, provides the linguistic foundation for the translation of Hegel into Italian, Spanish, French, or English. The translation, "veritas existentiae est essentia," would be utter nonsense. Missing in it would be the entire speculative movement voiced in the living German words and word relationships. In the *"Wahrheit"* of *"Wahrheit des Seins"* a multiplicity of things is heard which are not implied by *veritas:* authenticity, unconcealedness, genuineness, a thing's proving itself true, and so forth. In the same way, *Sein* is definitely not existence, nor is it being-there *(Dasein),* nor being something in particular *(etwas sein).* On the contrary, it is *Wesen,* precisely, but in the sense that both *Sein* and *Wesen* have the temporal character of verbs which have been made nominatives, but which at the same time evoke the movement captured in Heidegger's *"Anwesen."* Heidegger had good reason to select this statement of Hegel's for the discussion. He did so with the obvious intention of testing whether Hegel fails to listen to himself and instead forces that which the language suggests and reveals as the deeper insight, into the methodically rigorous logic of the developing dialectic. It is true that if one lets the language speak and if one listens to what it says, one hears in it something other than that which Hegel was able to conceptualize within the whole of his dialectic in the *Logic.* But that is not all. Beyond that, one immediately becomes aware of the fact that the statement in question is not so much a statement about *Wesen* as it is the language of *Wesen* itself speaking.

It can hardly be avoided that upon hearing this interpretation

---

the impossibility of finding an equivalent for these words in any other language. The last of these three, *Wesen,* is particularly problematic. Essence will not do, ultimately, for it lacks the verbal dimension of *Wesen.* Compare Heidegger's *Anwesen,* coming into presence. (TRANS.)

someone will say that the author is "Heideggering" or, to use the expression of the early twenties, is "Heideggerizing." But with equal justification one who is really at home in the German language can turn to Meister Eckhard, Jakob Böhme, Leibniz, or Franz von Bader for corroboration of the point I am making.

Let us take Heidegger's counter to Hegel: "Das Wesen des Daseins liegt in seiner Existenz."[3] It is well known that Sartre attempted to utilize this traditional sounding statement for the purposes of French existentialism by interpreting it in the traditional sense—and that in so doing he provoked a critical rebuttal from Heidegger. Heidegger was quick to point out that in the text of *Being and Time, Wesen* was placed in single quotation marks, which would reveal to the attentive reader that it was not to be taken here in the traditional sense of *essentia.* "Essentia hominis in existentia sua consistuit" is certainly not Heidegger though, at best, it might be Sartre. Today no one doubts that even then Heidegger looked upon *Wesen* as the temporal, verbal form of *Sein* and that he saw in *Sein* just as in *Wesen* the temporality of *Anwesen,* or drawing into presence. What we have said of Hegel above might be said of Heidegger too, namely, that his presence in our language does not consist in the specific terminology he coins. Indeed much of this terminology appears to have been a passing attempt to provoke thought rather than an enduring language which thought could be said to possess and repeat. But just as Hegel is able to conjure up speculative truths out of the simplest turns of speech in German, e.g., *an sich, für sich, an und für sich,* or from words like *Wahr-nehmung*[4] and *Bestimmung,*[5] so too Heidegger is constantly listening for the hidden message which language gives to thought. And both are thus fascinated by the splendid example of Heraclitus. Indeed, at the decisive point in the path his own thinking took, the point of the "turning," Heidegger dared to consciously incorporate Hölderlin's poetic language in the language of his own thinking. What became sayable for him as a result provides the firm ground, the soil from which his criticism of the language of metaphysics and his quite explicitly destructive treatment of traditional concepts grew

3. Something in the order of: "The essence (?) of being there lies in its existence." Perhaps "nature" would be a better choice than "essence," but the problem is certainly not solved by it. See note 2. (TRANS.)

4. Literally, "taking to be true," but in ordinary usage, "perceive." (TRANS.)

5. "Determination." (TRANS.)

to positive fruition. Precisely for that reason, however, he continuously found himself confronted with the problem of marking off his own attempts at thought from Hegel's—for Hegel's artistry with concepts grows out of the same speculative soil of the German language.

Heidegger's thought reflects specifically upon what language itself is. Thus, in opposition to the Greek *logos* philosophy, to which Hegel's method of self-consciousness is pledged, he advances a counter-thought. His criticism of dialectic takes aim at the fact that in dialectic the "speculative," "positive," and "reasonable" truth is taken as a presence *(Anwesenheit)* and is thus grounded in an absolute apprehension, be this *nous, intellectus agens,* or reason. This presence is supposed to be stated, and once formulated in the structure of a predicative statement, it is drawn into the play of incessant negation and sublimation of itself. That is dialectic. For Heidegger, who is not oriented towards speaking as it occurs in the form of a statement, but rather towards the temporalness of the presence itself which speaks to us, saying is always more a holding true to the whole of what is to be said and a holding back before what is unsaid.

For Greek metaphysical thought, the unconcealed was wrested from concealment, or put another way, *alētheia* was determined as the overcoming of *pseudos*. In Heidegger's opinion thinking of things in this way diminishes the reality of language. To be sure, one can say that since the days of Vico and Herder the development of modern science has been accompanied by a certain awareness of that to which Heidegger directs our attention. Still it was only after the new information theory had brought modern science to its perfection that the problem of the dependence (and relative independence) of our thought on (from) language came into full view. Disconcealment is not only essentially tied to concealment but also to the defining though hidden work of the latter: as language, to shelter "being" concealed within itself. Thought is dependent upon the ground of language insofar as language is not merely a system of signs for the purpose of communication and transmission of information. Where there is real language, the thing to be designated is not known prior to the act of designation. Rather within our language relationship to world, that which is spoken of is itself first articulated through language's constitutive structuring of our being in the world. Speaking remains tied to the language as a whole, the hermeneutic virtuality of discourse which surpasses at any moment that which has been said.

It is precisely in this respect that speaking always transcends the linguistically constituted realm within which we find ourselves. That is made evident, for example, in the encounter with foreign languages, particularly those of an entirely different historical and cultural origin, which introduce us to an experience of world which we had previously lacked and for which we had lacked the words. But we are dealing with language here nonetheless. In the final analysis that obtains as well for the experience of world which our surroundings continue to offer us, however much these might be made over into a world managed by technology. However far language might slip into a technical function, as language it holds the invariable things in our nature fast, those things which come to be spoken of in language again and again. And the language of philosophy, as long as it remains language, will remain a dialogue with that language of our world.

Index